# Personality Psychology, Ideology, and Voting Behavior: Beyond the Ballot

Ben F. Cotterill

# Personality Psychology, Ideology, and Voting Behavior: Beyond the Ballot

Ben F. Cotterill
Department of Psychology
Clemson University
Clemson, SC, USA

ISBN 978-3-031-39641-0          ISBN 978-3-031-39642-7   (eBook)
https://doi.org/10.1007/978-3-031-39642-7

This Palgrave Macmillan imprint is published by the registered company Springer Nature Switzerland AG.
The registered company address is: Gewerbestrasse 11, 6330 Cham, Switzerland

Paper in this product is recyclable.

# Contents

# List of Tables

# 1

# Introduction

**Abstract** Political attitudes influence vote choice and public policy in modern democracies. Therefore, it is useful to identify how political attitudes are developed. A growing literature has focused on personality traits as explanatory factors. While personality is only a piece of the puzzle, it can explain some of the variation in political orientations and deserves further examination.

**Keywords** Personality • Trait theory

As an instructor of a university course on personality psychology, one of the things I find most intriguing is how our biological temperament influences our political leanings. Despite the limited awareness of this research, the discoveries and implications are likely to be valuable to many individuals. This text aims to present the relevant research findings in a way that is clear and accessible, demonstrating why everyone perceives the world differently. By increasing our knowledge of others, it will be easier to deal with differences and conflicts. The goal is to explain how

© The Author(s), under exclusive license to Springer Nature Switzerland AG 2023

B. F. Cotterill, *Personality Psychology, Ideology, and Voting Behavior: Beyond the Ballot*, https://doi.org/10.1007/978-3-031-39642-7_1

people experience and interpret the political world and to illustrate how this is linked to inherent predispositions, with a specific focus on individual personalities.

When you think about a person's personality, you probably start by listing a few descriptions. For example, whether they're friendly, funny, or trustworthy. These concepts are labels we apply to what we think are relatively stable patterns of behavior. However, personality is much more complex than this, as it is comprised of a person's thoughts and emotions as well. There have been numerous personality theories proposed over the years. Depth psychologists, such as Sigmund Freud and Carl Jung, emphasized unconscious complexes or suppressed sexual desires when explaining personality. Neo-Freudians, including Alfred Adler and Karen Horney, focused on more conscious sources of motivation for personality, such as feelings of inferiority or attempts to ward-off anxiety. Following this, behaviorists and social learning theorists studied more observable causes of personality, including environmental reinforcements. Humanistic theorists, like Abraham Maslow and Carl Rogers, argued that people naturally strive for growth and happiness in their surroundings. More recently, trait theories have become more and more popular when studying personality, proposing that individuals think and act differently due to variations in the intensity of basic trait dimensions that remain stable over time.

It is clear that personality is influenced by a wide range of factors, including genetic predispositions (e.g., Borkenau et al., 2001; Forsman et al., 2010; Ruf et al., 2008), cultural and social norms (e.g., Choi et al., 2015), the parenting styles of one's parents and other family dynamics (e.g., Ang, 2006; Doinita & Maria, 2015; Karavasilis et al., 2003; Yap et al., 2014), peer relationships (e.g., Powers & Bierman, 2013), and numerous past experiences. Equally, it is clear that personality has a range of implications, such as influencing one's clothing preferences (e.g., Moody et al., 2010) and taste in music and movies (e.g., Hall, 2005). Later in the text, it will be demonstrated how researchers can predict people's political beliefs based upon their personality. Basically, our inbuilt personality acts as a set of filters that influence the way we perceive the world, altering how we process information and even how we vote.

As you will know, people do not encounter the world as if they were blank slates, in political contexts or otherwise. There are people who exhibit similar patterns of behavior throughout their entire lives, whether it be outgoingness, orderliness, shyness, or untidiness. These personality differences are a reflection of who we are as individuals, and to some extent, they are rooted in our biology (a topic that will be covered later in this text). These differences persist over extended periods, with certain sub-elements of personality, known as traits, being exceptionally stable. The trait-based approach to personality is currently the most popular in psychology, as it offers a theoretical framework for understanding personality and allows for empirical measurement. Kreitler and Kreitler (1990, p. 4) define a trait as "a relatively stable tendency or feature characteristic of an individual." For example, while introverts may occasionally behave like extraverts and vice versa, most individuals have a predisposition towards one behavior or the other in most situations.

Generally, extraverts tend to gain energy from social interactions, whereas introverts tend to become tired from social interactions. Personality, therefore, has an influence on the things we value. For instance, extraverts value socializing, while introverts value solitude. It may not seem surprising, therefore, that personality can also impact what we value when it comes to making political choices. For example, a more compassionate person may be likely to value policies with fairness and care for others at the core. Similarly, a more open individual may value diversity, while a socially responsible person may value order and respect for authority. It is important to demonstrate these ideas empirically, even if they do seem intuitive. Hopefully, this text will manage to do just that.

As will be demonstrated, personality traits are measured on a spectrum and there is a normal distribution, meaning that most people are near the middle, and very few people are at the extremes. While traits typically manifest early in life and are generally stable across the lifespan, it is possible for individuals to develop skills that expand beyond their natural tendencies. For example, an introverted person can learn to become more outgoing, while an extraverted individual can learn to enjoy their own company. Such personal growth is a sign of character or wisdom. However, it is important to note that while one may expand their domain of competence, they may still feel more comfortable in situations that align with their natural tendencies. This is true for other personality traits as well, and this text will demonstrate how various traits have an impact on political attitudes and values.

In modern democracies, it's evident that political attitudes have a significant impact on vote choice and public policy. Therefore, understanding the development of these attitudes is important, including why some individuals participate in political protests, what shapes their ideological beliefs, and what influences their stance on their country's openness. While personality traits have been studied as potential explanatory factors, it's important to note that they are just one aspect of a larger picture. Other factors such as socio-economic status and demographic characteristics also play a role. While personality traits alone do not determine political attitudes, they do account for a significant portion of the variation and are a noteworthy contributing factor worthy of further investigation.

# References

Ang, R. P. (2006). Effects of parenting style on personal and social variables for Asian adolescents. *American Journal of Orthopsychiatry, 76*(4), 503–511. https://doi.org/10.1037/0002-9432.76.4.503

Borkenau, P., Riemann, R., Angleitner, A., & Spinath, F. M. (2001). Genetic and environmental influences on observed personality: Evidence from the German observational study of adult twins. *Journal of Personality and Social Psychology, 80*(4), 655–668. https://doi.org/10.1037/0022-3514.80.4.655

Choi, D., Oh, I.-S., & Colbert, A. E. (2015). Understanding organizational commitment: A meta-analytic examination of the roles of the five-factor model of personality and culture. *Journal of Applied Psychology, 100*(5), 1542–1567. https://doi.org/10.1037/apl0000014

Doinita, N. E., & Maria, N. D. (2015). Attachment and parenting styles. *Procedia-Social and Behavioral Sciences, 203*, 199–204. https://doi.org/10.1016/j.sbspro.2015.08.282

Forsman, M., Lichtenstein, P., Andershed, H., & Larsson, H. (2010). A longitudinal twin study of the direction of effects between psychopathic personality and antisocial behaviour. *Journal of Child Psychology and Psychiatry, 51*(1), 39–47. https://doi.org/10.1111/j.1469-7610.2009.02141.x

Hall, A. (2005). Audience personality and the selection of media and media genres. *Media Psychology, 7*(4), 377–398. https://doi.org/10.1207/ S1532785XMEP0704_4

Karavasilis, L., Doyle, A. B., & Markiewicz, D. (2003). Associations between parenting style and attachment to mother in middle childhood and adolescence. *International Journal of Behavioral Development, 27*(2), 153–164. https://doi.org/10.1080/0165025024400015

Kreitler, S., & Kreitler, H. (1990). Traits: The embattled concept. In *The cognitive foundations of personality traits. Emotions, personality, and psychotherapy.* Springer. https://doi.org/10.1007/978-1-4899-2227-4_1

Moody, W., Kinderman, P., & Sinha, P. (2010). An exploratory study: Relationships between trying on clothing, mood, emotion, personality and clothing preference. *Journal of Fashion Marketing and Management: An International Journal, 14*(1), 161–179. https://doi.org/10.1108/1361 2021011025483

Powers, C. J., Bierman, K. L., & The Conduct Problems Prevention Research Group. (2013). The multifaceted impact of peer relations on aggressive–disruptive behavior in early elementary school. *Developmental Psychology, 49*(6), 1174–1186. https://doi.org/10.1037/a0028400

Ruf, H. T., Schmidt, N. L., Lemery-Chalfant, K., & Goldsmith, H. H. (2008). Components of childhood impulsivity and inattention: Child, family, and genetic correlates. *European Journal of Developmental Science, 2*(1–2), 52–76. https://doi.org/10.3233/DEV-2008-21205

Yap, M. B. H., Pilkington, P. D., Ryan, S. M., & Jorm, A. F. (2014). Parental factors associated with depression and anxiety in young people: A systematic review and meta-analysis. *Journal of Affective Disorders, 156*, 8–23. https:// doi.org/10.1016/j.jad.2013.11.007

# Part I

Personality

# 2

# The Big Five

**Abstract** This chapter summarizes the academic research on personality traits, beginning with Gordon Allport's lexical approach in 1936 and explaining how it led to the emergence of the Big Five Model (Openness, Conscientiousness, Extraversion, Agreeableness, and Neuroticism), now widely endorsed by psychologists. Additionally, this chapter explores how psychologists can predict specific outcomes based on the scores obtained by participants in questionnaires designed to evaluate these five personality dimensions.

**Keywords** Personality • Trait theory • Big Five • Openness • Conscientiousness • Extraversion • Agreeableness • Neuroticism

At the start of the twentieth century, Gordon Allport's lexical hypothesis built upon the premise that natural languages would have evolved terms for all fundamental personality differences (McCrae & Costa, 1985a). In 1936, Allport and Odbert identified 18,000 personality-descriptive terms from an English language dictionary. To narrow down the list, Allport

© The Author(s), under exclusive license to Springer Nature Switzerland AG 2023    **9**
B. F. Cotterill, *Personality Psychology, Ideology, and Voting Behavior: Beyond the Ballot*,
https://doi.org/10.1007/978-3-031-39642-7_2

excluded evaluative words, such as "good" and "bad," and focused on words that could apply across cultures and those with a higher number of synonyms. He extracted 4500 words for his final list of personality traits.

In 1946, Raymond Cattell noticed similarities between words in Allport's list, and theorized that personality traits could be condensed into a smaller number of words. He used the emerging technology of computers to analyze Allport's list of personality traits, employing the technique known as factor analysis—a statistical approach to understanding and analyzing data. He organized the list into 181 clusters, and asked participants to rate people whom they knew based upon the traits on the list. By using factor analysis, he reduced these 181 clusters into what he thought were the 16 most basic and central traits, which he referred to as source traits.

Cattell's factor analysis approach revolutionized personality psychology. It allowed researchers to statistically determine how similar adjectives are to one another (at least in regard to how those adjectives are used to describe the fundamental differences between people). For example, if a group of 1000 people were asked to describe themselves using a list of adjectives that included "compassionate" and "altruistic," it would become clear that those who rated themselves high on one trait tended to rate themselves high on the other as well, and vice versa for those who rated themselves low on both traits. By analyzing these patterns of covariation, researchers could identify the fundamental dimensions of human personality. Although compassion and altruism are distinct traits, they are similar enough to suggest that they share an underlying dimension that differentiates people.

Since Raymond Cattell's first use of factor analysis, personality psychologists have continued to use the technique to decide how many fundamental traits exist (i.e., how many out of the thousands in the dictionary are truly essential). The Big Five is currently the most widely accepted answer. These five traits are Openness (tendency to be curious and unconventional), Conscientiousness (tendency to be organized and disciplined), Extraversion (tendency to be outgoing and enthusiastic), Agreeableness (tendency to be sympathetic and cooperative), and Neuroticism (tendency to be anxious and insecure). They can be remembered using the acronym OCEAN.

Donald Fiske, in 1949, was likely the first researcher to identify the emergence of these five traits through factor analysis. In 1961, Tupes and Christal found the same five factors after examining personality scores from eight different samples, including graduate students and Air Force personnel. The finding that these five factors best resemble the structure of personality was reaffirmed by Norman in 1963, as well as several scholars who developed questionnaires with single-word person-adjectives in order to measure personality (e.g., Digman, 1990, as cited in Goldberg, 1993; Digman & Inouye, 1986; Goldberg, 1990, 1992, 1993; Fiske, 1949, as cited in Schultz & Schultz, 2005; Norman, 1963; Tupes & Christal, 1961, as cited in Goldberg, 1993; Saucier & Goldberg, 1996). In 1996, Saucier and Goldberg found the same five traits after analyzing results of nearly a thousand participants. At first, the basis of these five traits was questionable, but the Big Five have been found again and again over the years, using many different lists of traits and wide ranges of people as subjects. One reason the Big Five has become so popular is that when personality tests (not just words in the dictionary) are factor analyzed, a common finding is that they, too, tend to fall into groups defined by the Big Five. This model, therefore, can be viewed as an integration rather than an opponent of other trait approaches.

Some researchers have suggested that the Big Five be referred to by Roman numerals I–V, because the labels are not useful (Funder, 2019). This is because they are necessarily oversimplified and potentially misleading. Importantly, each of the five factors are "not so much one thing but more of a collection of many things that have something in common" (Saucier & Goldberg, 2003, p. 14). In order to combat this problem, Costa and McCrae divided each of the Big Five into six facets. Costa and McCrae's Revised NEO Personality Inventory (or NEO PI-R) is currently the most popular method of assessing the Big Five (Soto & John, 2009). As opposed to the single-word person-adjectives used to measure the five factors, the NEO PI-R uses short sentences to measure the Big Five and facets. It contains 240 items and six subcategories for each of the five factors (see Table 2.1). The subcategories are referred to by the authors as lower order facets, representing the distinct, though co-varying, elements within a trait (Costa & McCrae, 1995). They limited the number of facets to six because they felt "more than six would soon lead to

**Table 2.1** Facets of the Big Five in Costa and McCrae's NEO PI-R

| Openness | Conscientiousness | Extraversion | Agreeableness | Neuroticism |
|---|---|---|---|---|
| Imagination | Competence | Warmth | Trust | Anxiety |
| Artistic interest | Orderliness | Gregariousness | Straight forwardness | Hostility |
| Emotionality | Dutifulness | Assertiveness | Altruism | Depression |
| Exploration | Achievement striving | Lively temperament | Compliance | Self-consciousness |
| Intellectual interest | Self-discipline | Excitement seeking | Modesty | Impulsiveness |
| Tolerance to ambiguity | Cautiousness | Positive emotions | Sympathy | Vulnerability to stress |

intellectual overload" (Costa & McCrae, 1995, pp. 26–27). These facets have shown important information about individual differences beyond the level of the Big Five.

The test has proven to have high internal consistency, to produce stable responses across time, and to be valid with children (Markey et al., 2004). A great deal of cross-cultural research has also been carried out using the NEO PI-R, finding robust evidence through factor analysis of the Big Five in China, Estonia, Finland, France, German-speaking countries, India, Mexico, Portugal, Russia, South Korean, the Philippines, Turkey, Vietnam, and Zimbabwe, as well as 51 further countries (McCrae & Terracciano, 2005). However, it should be noted that studies have failed to replicate the five-factor structure in some parts of the world, such as with an indigenous society in the Amazon (Gurven et al., 2013).

Although the same factors are common to many cultures, there are major differences in regard to their relative importance (Allik & McCrae, 2004; McCrae & Terracciano, 2005). Japanese residents consider Conscientiousness to be more important than all the other factors. In Hong Kong and India, Agreeableness was found to be the most important factor. In Australia, Extraversion and Agreeableness are considered to be more desirable than the other three factors. Overall, Europeans and Americans tend to score higher in Extraversion and Openness and lower in Agreeableness compared to Asians and Africans. The distribution of personality traits also varies depending on geographical location in the United States. For example, agreeable people are more likely to be found in the South-eastern United States, and Openness is highest in areas near Denver, Los Angeles, Miami, New York City, Portland, San Antonio, Seattle, and San Francisco (Florida, 2008, as cited in Funder, 2019).

Around the world, sex differences vary geographically as well. In general, women score higher than men on Agreeableness, Extraversion, Neuroticism, and Orderliness (an aspect of Conscientiousness), while men score higher in Industriousness (an aspect of Conscientiousness), though the difference in Extraversion is only slight, and the difference in Neuroticism only appears after the onset of puberty. These differences are more significant in wealthier, more egalitarian countries, particularly in the Netherlands, Norway, Sweden, Germany, the UK, Canada, the United States, Australia, and France (in that order, with the Netherlands reporting the highest sex differences). In contrast, China has reported the lowest sex differences, followed by Malaysia, South Korea, and Japan (Giolla & Kajonius, 2019).

The Big Five personality traits can be identified through factor analysis using questionnaires not even designed to measure the five factors, including Cattell's 16PF and the Eysenck Personality Questionnaire. For instance, the traits Extraversion and Neuroticism of Eysenck's Personality Questionnaire are represented in the traits Extraversion and Neuroticism of the Big Five, while the third personality trait of Eysenck's model, Psychoticism, is represented in the traits Agreeableness and Conscientiousness (Aluja et al., 2002; Digman, 1997; Goldberg, 1993; Markon et al., 2005; McCrae & Costa, 1985b, 1987). There is also a considerable degree of consistency between self-ratings and observer-ratings of the Big Five traits, further supporting their reliability (Connolly et al., 2007; Costa & McCrae, 1986, 1988).

One of the biggest criticisms of the Big Five is that it leaves out important aspects of personality. Critics have claimed that there are missing traits, such as egotism, manipulativeness, honesty, sexiness/seductiveness, thriftiness, masculinity/femininity, snobbishness, sense of humor, and risk-taking/thrill-seeking (Ashton et al., 2004; Ashton & Lee, 2008; Di Blas, 2005; Lanning, 1994; Lee & Ashton, 2008; Paunonen, 2002, as cited in Larsen & Buss, 2001; Paunonen et al., 2003; Saucier et al., 2005). Some of these constructs are correlative with the five factors. For instance, honesty correlates with Agreeableness. However, critics argue that much of the individual variation is left unaccounted for, suggesting that these individual differences are not completely subsumed by the five-factor model. Proponents of the five-factor model are typically open minded about the potential inclusion of factors beyond the Big Five, if and when the empirical evidence warrants it. Nonetheless, these researchers have not found the evidence for additional factors so far to be compelling.

Though not all psychologists accept McCrae and Costa's factors, the Big Five remains the most popular trait approach among personality researchers. Some researchers have proposed more than five personality dimensions, and others have argued that no list of factors can fully describe the complexity of human personality. Nonetheless, the Big Five has been widely replicated and has inspired a great deal of research. Another strength of the Big Five is that results are generally stable. Openness is especially stable across the lifespan, along with certain elements of Extraversion such as sociability, positive affect, gregariousness, and energy level. Social dominance (or Assertiveness, an aspect of Extraversion), Agreeableness, Conscientiousness, and Emotional Stability tend to increase across the lifespan (for a review, see Roberts et al., 2006). There is also biological evidence provided for the existence of the five traits, explored in more detail in the next chapter.

The biggest strength of the model is its ability to predict future behavior. For example, Conscientiousness is a strong predictor of having a healthy lifestyle and living longer (Connor-Smith & Flashbart, 2007; Tucker et al., 2006; Walton & Roberts, 2004). This is because conscientious people are less likely to engage in negative health behaviors, such as drinking alcohol, drug use, and smoking. Furthermore, they are more likely to engage in positive health behaviors, such as exercising and dieting. Longitudinal studies, some investigating the same people for nearly 70 years, have shown that children scoring higher in Conscientiousness are more likely to be physically healthier in adulthood, and to live longer than children who scored lower in Conscientiousness (Booth-Kewley & Vickers, 1994; Friedman et al., 1993, 1995; Marshall et al., 1994).

Another popular method of dividing the Big Five is the Big Five Aspect Scales by DeYoung et al. (2007), which separates the five factors into two aspects. According to this approach: Openness is made up of

Openness-to-experience and Intellect, Conscientiousness is made up of Orderliness and Industriousness, Extraversion is made up of Enthusiasm and Assertiveness, Agreeableness is made up of Politeness and Compassion, and Neuroticism is made up of Withdrawal and Volatility. Each of the Big Five will now be explained in detail.

Openness reflects aesthetic sensitivity, creativity, and intellectual curiosity (McCrae, 1987; Weisberg et al., 2011; Ziegler et al., 2015). It is a predictor of divergent thinking and creative achievement (Batey & Furnham, 2006; Carson et al., 2003; Feist, 1998; Feist & Barron, 2003; King et al., 1996; Kaufman et al., 2016; McCrae, 1987; Silvia et al., 2009). People who score high in Openness typically enjoy experiencing new things and have a fascination with fiction, art, movies, poetry, philosophical discussions, and non-mainstream music. They are also more likely to engage in imaginative thinking, have a curious mind, and be interested in exploring different cultures (Schwaba et al. 2018; Zhiyan & Singer, 1997). DeYoung's (2006) model divides Openness into two aspects: Openness-to-experience and Intellect. These two aspects independently predict separate outcomes. For example, Intellect predicts general intelligence, as well as verbal and nonverbal intelligence, while Openness-to-experience is only associated with verbal intelligence (DeYoung et al., 2014). Openness-to-experience is positively related to an increased interest in novel stimuli, while Intellect is predictive of increased understanding of such stimuli (DeYoung et al., 2014). Individuals who score high in Openness are typically lower in dogmatism and have a reduced need for cognitive closure (Mondak & Halperin, 2008; Onraet et al., 2011).

Conscientiousness is associated with self-discipline and organization (Weisberg et al., 2011). Therefore, conscientious people tend to be more organized, and less cluttered in their homes and workplaces than people scoring lower in Conscientiousness. They are more likely to have their books at home neatly shelved in alphabetical order or categorized by topic, and to have their clothes folded and arranged in drawers. Conscientiousness is the best personality predictor of success in education (Dumfart & Neubauer, 2016), sometimes even accounting for a larger portion of the variance than intelligence (Kappe & van der Flier, 2012). This is likely because conscientious people are more likely to attend classes and to submit assignments on time. Furthermore, industrious people tend to make efficient use of their time, find inactivity adverse, and are more likely to experience guilt as a result of using their time unproductively (Kertechian, 2018). According to DeYoung's (2006) model, Conscientiousness is divided into Orderliness and Industriousness. Orderly people are more likely to be higher in disgust sensitivity, meaning they find mess and dirt intolerable (Xu et al., 2016). They are less likely than disorderly people to discuss sexual matters with friends, lounge around the house without any clothes on, pick up a hitch-hiker, ride in a car without a seatbelt, swear around other people, or tell a dirty joke (Hirsh et al., 2009).

The concept of Extraversion was first introduced by Carl Jung (1921, as cited in Jung, 2014), referring to whether one orientates themselves towards external (e.g., socializing) or internal experiences (e.g., reading, thinking). However, Jung's observations have been criticized for only being based upon those in his own life (Boeree, 2006). Nowadays, Extraversion is commonly characterized in terms of sociability and outgoingness (Costa & McCrae, 1992), though it also involves assertiveness (DeYoung et al., 2007; Goldberg, 1992; Shiner & DeYoung, 2013) and one's tendency to experience positive emotions (Depue & Collins, 1999; Gray & McNaughton, 2003; Robinson et al., 2010; Tellegen et al., 1988). Extraversion is relatively stable across the lifespan and has a powerful impact on behavior (Roberts et al., 2006). For example, it is quite difficult for introverts to act like extraverts, and vice versa. Extraverts report higher levels of happiness and are more sensitive to rewards (Gray, 1970, as cited in Gray & McNaughton, 2003). They are also more likely to have a higher number of sexual partners and to have children at a younger age (Eysenck & Eysenck, 1975, as cited in Larsen & Buss, 2001). Extraverts are more likely to process their thoughts externally, seek out time for socializing, and to have a larger variety of friends (Asendorpf & Wilpers, 1998). Introverts, on the other hand, typically dislike being the center of attention, avoid large groups, are more emotionally reserved, and are more likely to seek time alone to think and recharge (Duffy et al., 2018). According to DeYoung's (2006) model, Extraversion is divided into Assertiveness and Enthusiasm, described by DeYoung (2010) as the difference between "wanting" and "liking" a reward.

Agreeableness is associated with being self-sacrificing, compassionate, and polite (DeYoung et al., 2007). Highly agreeable people will put another person's concerns ahead of their own. They are generally altruistic, compliant, cooperative, empathetic, modest, non-competitive, and conflict-averse (Costa & McCrae, 1992; Weisberg et al., 2011). According to DeYoung's (2006) model, Agreeableness is divided into Compassion and Politeness. Low Agreeableness is a predictor of deviant behavior (Salgado, 2002; Vize et al., 2016). High Agreeableness is an indicator of lower income (Matz & Gladstone, 2020). This may be because they are less likely to ask for pay rises in the first place and are also less likely to be competent negotiators. Disagreeable people are argumentative and like to have everything their own way without regard for others. Extremely low Agreeableness is predictive of many personality disorders, including narcissism and psychopathy (Vernon et al., 2008). As is the case with any trait, very few people score extremely high or low. Instead, most people score near the middle of the spectrum, leaning one way a little more than the other (Funder, 2019). Along with Neuroticism, Agreeableness is one of the two Big Five dimensions with the largest and most reliably reported sex differences, with women tending to score higher than men on both (Costa et al., 2001; Feingold, 1994; Weisberg et al., 2011), though, as previously mentioned, significant sex differences in Neuroticism do not emerge until adolescence (Parker & Brotchie, 2010).

Neuroticism is associated with tendencies to experience negative emotion, including anger, anxiety, depression, and self-consciousness (Kale et al., 2020; Weisberg et al., 2011). Individuals who score high on Neuroticism are more likely to report lower self-esteem, and to be shyer and more self-conscious (Judge et al. 1998). They are also more at risk for developing common mental disorders, such as mood disorders and anxiety disorders (Jeronimus et al., 2016). Highly neurotic people are particularly sensitive to threats, including social threats, such as a fear that they may not be accepted or liked by others. There is a negative correlation between Neuroticism and happiness, wellbeing, and physical health (Connor-Smith & Flashbart, 2007; DeNeve & Cooper, 1998). In DeYoung's (2006) model, Neuroticism is made of Withdrawal and Volatility. The distinction is linked to Gray and McNaughton's (2000, as cited in Shiner & DeYoung, 2013) theory that Neuroticism is linked to two systems—the behavioral inhibition system (BIS) and the fight-flight-freeze system (FFFS). The FFFS, involving the amygdala and lower regions of the brain, responds to threatening stimuli in terms of flight (panic) or fight (reactive aggression). The BIS, on the other hand, centered around the hippocampus, responds to stimuli that one desires but that contains threat, creating an approach-avoidance conflict (Shiner & DeYoung, 2013), such as wanting to ask someone on a date but fearing rejection or wanting to impress your teacher with a presentation but being worried about judgment from peers. Clearly, the anger or panic, connected to the FFFS, is reflected in Volatility, while anxiety and self-consciousness, connected to the BIS, is reflected in Withdrawal.

Many life outcomes are best predicted by combinations of personality dispositions, rather than by one personality trait alone. For instance:

- Good grades in school are predicted by high Conscientiousness and low Neuroticism (Chamorro-Premuzic & Furnham, 2003);
- Risky sexual behaviors are predicted by high Extraversion, high Neuroticism, low Conscientiousness, and low Agreeableness (Allen & Walter, 2018; Miller et al., 2004; Trobst et al., 2002; Zietsch et al., 2010);
- High alcohol consumption is predicted by high Extraversion and low Conscientiousness (Paunonen, 2003);
- Pathological gambling is predicted by high Neuroticism and low Conscientiousness (Bagby et al., 2007);
- Volunteering is predicted by high Agreeableness and high Extraversion (Carlo et al., 2005);
- Declining to become a union member at work is predicted by low Extraversion and low Neuroticism (Parkes & Razavi, 2004);
- Forgiveness is predicted by high Agreeableness and low Neuroticism (Brose et al., 2005);
- Leadership effectiveness is predicted by high Extraversion, high Agreeableness, high Conscientiousness, and low Neuroticism (Hassan et al., 2016; Silverthorne, 2001);
- Compliance with social distancing guidelines during the COVID-19 pandemic in 2020 was predicted by high Conscientiousness and high Neuroticism (Abdelrahman, 2020; Aschwanden et al., 2021).

# Summary

Costa and McCrae proposed five biologically based factors of personality: Openness, Conscientiousness, Extraversion, Agreeableness, and Neuroticism. Each person exhibits a unique combination of trait patterns. The factors are stable over a person's lifetime and appear in many cultures. They are valid predictors of behaviors, and have implications in the workplace, as well as in fields of health and therapy. Costa and McCrae's NEO PI-R is the most commonly used method of assessing the Big Five, and results have proven to be consistent. Additionally, the Big Five Aspects Scale is another popular tool that divides each of the Big Five factors into two aspects, both of which have the capacity to forecast separate behaviors and outcomes.

# Exercises

- You may complete the Big Five Aspects Scale here: https://bigfiveaspects.com/. Consider if your results represent your personality and if you feel the model is a useful method for studying personality.

# References

Abdelrahman, M. (2020). Personality traits, risk perception, and protective behaviors of Arab residents of Qatar during the COVID-19 pandemic. *International Journal of Mental Health Addiction, 20*, 237. https://doi.org/10.1007/s11469-020-00352-7

Allik, J., & McCrae, R. R. (2004). Toward a geography of personality traits: Patterns of profiles across 36 cultures. *Journal of Cross-Cultural Psychology, 35*(1), 13–28. https://doi.org/10.1177/0022022103260382

Allen, M. S., & Walter, E. E. (2018). Linking big five personality traits to sexuality and sexual health: A meta-analytic review. *Psychological Bulletin, 144*(10), 1081–1110. https://doi.org/10.1037/bul0000157

Aluja, A., Garcıa, Ó., & Garćıa, L. F. (2002). A comparative study of Zuckerman's three' structural models for personality through the NEO-PI-R, ZKPQ-III-R,

EPQ-RS and Goldberg's 50-bipolar adjectives. *Personality and Individual Differences, 33*(5), 713–725. https://doi.org/10.1016/S0191-8869(01)00186-6

Aschwanden, D., Strickhouser, J. E., Sesker, A. A., Lee, J. H., Luchetti, M., Stephan, Y., Sutin, A. R., & Terracciano, A. (2021). Psychological and behavioural responses to coronavirus disease 2019: The role of personality. *European Journal of Personality, 35*(1), 51–66. https://doi.org/10.1002/per.2281

Ashton, M. C., & Lee, K. (2008). The prediction of honesty–humility-related criteria by the HEXACO and five-factor models of personality. *Journal of Research in Personality, 42*(5), 1216–1228. https://doi.org/10.1016/j.jrp.2008.03.006

Ashton, M. C., Lee, K., Perugini, M., Szarota, P., de Vries, R. E., Di Blas, L., Boies, K., & De Raad, B. (2004). A six-factor structure of personality-descriptive adjectives: Solutions from Psycholexical studies in seven languages. *Journal of Personality and Social Psychology, 86*(2), 356–366. https://doi.org/10.1037/0022-3514.86.2.356

Asendorpf, J. B., & Wilpers, S. (1998). Personality effects on social relationships. *Journal of Personality and Social Psychology, 74*(6), 1531–1544. https://doi.org/10.1037/0022-3514.74.6.1531

Bagby, R. M., Vachon, D. D., Bulmash, E. L., Toneatto, T., Quilty, L. C., & Costa, P. T. (2007). Pathological gambling and the five-factor model of personality. *Personality and Individual Differences, 43*(4), 873–880. https://doi.org/10.1016/j.paid.2007.02.011

Batey, M., & Furnham, A. (2006). Creativity, intelligence, and personality: A critical review of the scattered literature. *Genetic, Social, and General Psychology Monographs, 132*(4), 355–429. https://doi.org/10.3200/MONO.132.4.355-430

Boeree, C. G. (2006). *Personality theories*. Retrieved March 4th, 2023 at http://webspace.ship.edu/cgboer/persintro.

Booth-Kewley, S., & Vickers, R. R., Jr. (1994). Associations between major domains of personality and health behavior. *Journal of Personality, 62*(3), 281–298. https://doi.org/10.1111/j.1467-6494.1994.tb00298.x

Brose, L. A., Rye, M. S., Lutz-Zois, C., & Ross, S. R. (2005). Forgiveness and personality traits. *Personality and Individual Differences, 39*(1), 35–46. https://doi.org/10.1016/j.paid.2004.11.001

Carlo, G., Okun, M. A., Knight, G. P., & de Guzman, M. R. T. (2005). The interplay of traits and motives on volunteering: Agreeableness, extraversion and prosocial value motivation. *Personality and Individual Differences, 38*(6), 1293–1305. https://doi.org/10.1016/j.paid.2004.08.012

Carson, S. H., Peterson, J. B., & Higgins, D. M. (2003). Decreased latent inhibition is associated with increased creative achievement in high-functioning individuals. *Journal of Personality and Social Psychology, 85*(3), 499–506. https://doi.org/10.1037/0022-3514.85.3.499

Chamorro-Premuzic, T., & Furnham, A. (2003). Personality predicts academic performance: Evidence from two longitudinal university samples. *Journal of Research in Personality, 37*(4), 319–338. https://doi.org/10.1016/S0092-6566(02)00578-0

Connolly, J. J., Kavanagh, E. J., & Viswesvaran, C. (2007). The convergent validity between self and observer ratings of personality: A meta-analytic review. *International Journal of Selection and Assessment, 15*(1), 110–117. https://doi.org/10.1111/j.1468-2389.2007.00371.x

Connor-Smith, J. K., & Flachsbart, C. (2007). Relations between personality and coping: A meta-analysis. *Journal of Personality and Social Psychology, 93*(6), 1080–1107. https://doi.org/10.1037/0022-3514.93.6.1080

Costa, P. T., & McCrae, R. R. (1986). Cross-sectional studies of personality in a national sample: I. Development and validation of survey measures. *Psychology and Aging, 1*(2), 140–143. https://doi.org/10.1037/0882-7974.1.2.140

Costa, P. T., & McCrae, R. R. (1988). Personality in adulthood: A six-year longitudinal study of self-reports and spouse ratings on the NEO personality inventory. *Journal of Personality and Social Psychology, 54*(5), 853–863. https://doi.org/10.1037/0022-3514.54.5.853

Costa, P. T., & McCrae, R. R. (1992). *NEO PI-R professional manual.* Psychological Assessment Resources.

Costa, P. T., & McCrae, R. R. (1995). Domains and facets: Hierarchical personality assessment using the revised NEO personality inventory. *Journal of Personality Assessment, 64*(1), 21–50. https://doi.org/10.1207/s15327752jpa6401_2

Costa, P. T., Jr., Terracciano, A., & McCrae, R. R. (2001). Gender differences in personality traits across cultures: Robust and surprising findings. *Journal of Personality and Social Psychology, 81*(2), 322. https://doi.org/10.1037/0022-3514.81.2.322

DeNeve, K. M., & Cooper, H. (1998). The happy personality: A meta-analysis of 137 personality traits and subjective well-being. *Psychological Bulletin, 124*(2), 197–229. https://doi.org/10.1037/0033-2909.124.2.197

Depue, R. A., & Collins, P. F. (1999). Neurobiology of the structure of personality: Dopamine, facilitation of incentive motivation, and extraversion. *Behavioral and Brain Sciences, 22*(3), 491–517. https://doi.org/10.1017/S0140525X99372046

DeYoung, C. G. (2006). Higher-order factors of the big five in a multi-informant sample. *Journal of Personality and Social Psychology, 91*(6), 1138–1151. https://doi.org/10.1037/0022-3514.91.6.1138

DeYoung, C. G. (2010). Personality neuroscience and the biology of traits. *Social and Personality Psychology Compass, 4*(12), 1165–1180. https://doi.org/10.1111/j.1751-9004.2010.00327.x

DeYoung, C. G., Quilty, L. C., & Peterson, J. B. (2007). Between facets and domains: 10 aspects of the big five. *Journal of Personality and Social Psychology, 93*(5), 880–896. https://doi.org/10.1037/0022-3514.93.5.880

DeYoung, C. G., Quilty, L. C., Peterson, J. B., & Gray, J. R. (2014). Openness to experience, intellect, and cognitive ability. *Journal of Personality Assessment, 96*(1), 46–52. https://doi.org/10.1080/00223891.2013.806627

Di Blas, L. (2005). Personality-relevant attribute-nouns: A taxonomic study in the Italian language. *European Journal of Personality: Published for the European Association of Personality Psychology, 19*(7), 537–557. https://doi.org/10.1002/per.569

Digman, J. M. (1997). Higher-order factors of the big five. *Journal of Personality and Social Psychology, 73*(6), 1246–1256. https://doi.org/10.1037/0022-3514.73.6.1246

Digman, J. M., & Inouye, J. (1986). Further specification of the five robust factors of personality. *Journal of Personality and Social Psychology, 50*(1), 116–123. https://doi.org/10.1037/0022-3514.50.1.116

Duffy, K. A., Helzer, E. G., Hoyle, R. H., Fukukura Helzer, J., & Chartrand, T. L. (2018). Pessimistic expectations and poorer experiences: The role of (low) extraversion in anticipated and experienced enjoyment of social interaction. *PLoS One, 13*(7), e0199146. https://doi.org/10.1371/journal.pone.0199146

Dumfart, B., & Neubauer, A. C. (2016). Conscientiousness is the most powerful noncognitive predictor of school achievement in adolescents. *Journal of Individual Differences, 37*(1), 8–15. https://doi.org/10.1027/1614-0001/a000182

Feingold, A. (1994). Gender differences in personality: A meta-analysis. *Psychological Bulletin, 116*(3), 429–456. https://doi.org/10.1037/0033-2909.116.3.429

Feist, G. J. (1998). A meta-analysis of personality in scientific and artistic creativity. *Personality and Social Psychology Review, 2*(4), 290–309. https://doi.org/10.1207/s15327957pspr0204_5

Feist, G. J., & Barron, F. X. (2003). Predicting creativity from early to late adulthood: Intellect, potential, and personality. *Journal of Research in Personality, 37*(2), 62–88. https://doi.org/10.1016/S0092-6566(02)00536-6

Friedman, H. S., Tucker, J. S., Schwartz, J. E., Martin, L. R., Tomlinson-Keasey, C., Wingard, D. L., & Criqui, M. H. (1995). Childhood conscientiousness and longevity: Health behaviors and cause of death. *Journal of Personality and Social Psychology, 68*(4), 696–703. https://doi.org/10.1037//0022-3514.68.4.696

Friedman, H. S., Tucker, J. S., Tomlinson-Keasey, C., Schwartz, J. E., Wingard, D. L., & Criqui, M. H. (1993). Does childhood personality predict longevity? *Journal of Personality and Social Psychology, 65*(1), 176–185. https://doi.org/10.1037//0022-3514.65.1.176

Funder, D. C. (2019). *The personality puzzle* (8th ed.). W. W. Norton & Company.

Giolla, E. M., & Kajonius, P. J. (2019). Sex differences in personality are larger in gender equal countries: Replicating and extending a surprising finding. *International Journal of Psychology, 54*(6), 705–711. https://doi.org/10.1002/ijop.12529

Goldberg, L. R. (1990). An alternative "description of personality": The big-five factor structure. *Journal of Personality and Social Psychology, 59*(6), 1216–1229. https://doi.org/10.1037/0022-3514.59.6.1216

Goldberg, L. R. (1992). The development of markers for the big-five factor structure. *Psychological Assessment, 4*(1), 26–42. https://doi.org/10.1037/1040-3590.4.1.26

Goldberg, L. R. (1993). The structure of phenotypic personality traits. *American Psychologist, 48*(1), 26–34. https://doi.org/10.1037/0003-066X.48.1.26

Gray, J. A., & McNaughton, N. (2003). *The neuropsychology of anxiety: An enquiry into the functions of the septo-hippocampal system* (2nd ed.). Oxford University Press.

Gurven, M., Von Rueden, C., Massenkoff, M., Kaplan, H., & Lero Vie, M. (2013). How universal is the big five? Testing the five-factor model of personality variation among forager–farmers in the Bolivian Amazon. *Journal of Personality and Social Psychology, 104*(2), 354–370. https://doi.org/10.1037/a0030841

Hassan, H., Asad, S., & Hoshino, Y. (2016). Determinants of leadership style in big five personality dimensions. *Universal Journal of Management, 4*(4), 161–179. https://doi.org/10.13189/ujm.2016.040402

Hirsh, J. B., DeYoung, C. G., & Peterson, J. B. (2009). Metatraits of the big five differentially predict engagement and restraint of behavior. *Journal of Personality, 77*(4), 1085–1102. https://doi.org/10.1111/j.1467-6494. 2009.00575.x

Jeronimus, B. F., Kotov, R., Riese, H., & Ormel, J. (2016). Neuroticism's prospective association with mental disorders halves after adjustment for baseline symptoms and psychiatric history, but the adjusted association hardly decays with time: A metaanalysis on 59 longitudinal/prospective studies with 443 313 participants. *Psychological Medicine, 46*(14), 2883–2906. https://doi. org/10.1017/S0033291716001653

Judge, T. A., Locke, E. A., Durham, C. C., & Kluger, A. N. (1998). Dispositional effects on job and life satisfaction: The role of core evaluations. *Journal of Applied Psychology, 83*(1), 17–34. https://doi.org/10.1037/0021-9010. 83.1.17

Jung, C. G. (2014). *Psychological types*. Routledge.

Kale, P., Inamdar, M., Shimpi, P., & Jha, P. (2020). Personality assessment tool using artificial intelligence: A review. *International Journal of Progressive Research in Science and Engineering, 1*(3), 104–107.

Kappe, R., & Van Der Flier, H. (2012). Predicting academic success in higher education: what's more important than being smart? *European Journal of Psychology of Education, 27*(4), 605–619. https://doi.org/10.1007/s10212-011-0099-9

Kaufman, S. B., Quilty, L. C., Grazioplene, R. G., Hirsh, J. B., Gray, J. R., Peterson, J. B., & DeYoung, C. G. (2016). Openness to experience and intellect differentially predict creative achievement in the arts and sciences. *Journal of Personality, 84*(2), 248–258. https://doi.org/10.1111/jopy.12156

Kertechian, S. K. (2018). Conscientiousness as a key to success for academic achievement among French university students enrolled in management studies. *The International Journal of Management Education, 16*(2), 154–165. https://doi.org/10.1016/j.ijme.2018.02.003

King, L. A., Walker, L. M., & Broyles, S. J. (1996). Creativity and the five-factor model. *Journal of Research in Personality, 30*(2), 189–203. https://doi. org/10.1006/jrpe.1996.0013

Lanning, K. (1994). Dimensionality of observer ratings on the California adult Q-set. *Journal of Personality and Social Psychology, 67*(1), 151–160. https:// doi.org/10.1037/0022-3514.67.1.151

Larsen, R. J., & Buss, D. M. (2001). *Personality psychology: Domains of knowledge about human nature* (3rd ed.). McGraw-Hill.

Lee, K., & Ashton, M. C. (2008). The HEXACO personality factors in the indigenous personality lexicons of English and 11 other languages. *Journal of Personality,* 76(5), 1001–1054. https://doi.org/10.1111/j.1467-6494.2008.00512.x

Markey, P., Markey, C., & Tinsley, B. (2004). Children's behavioral manifestations of the five-factor model of personality. *Personality and Social Psychology Bulletin, 30,* 423–432. https://doi.org/10.1177/0146167203261886

Markon, K. E., Krueger, R. F., & Watson, D. (2005). Delineating the structure of Normal and abnormal personality: An integrative hierarchical approach. *Journal of Personality and Social Psychology,* 88(1), 139–157. https://doi.org/10.1037/0022-3514.88.1.139

Marshall, G. N., Wortman, C. B., Vickers, R. R., Kusulas, J. W., & Hervig, L. K. (1994). The five-factor model of personality as a framework for personality-health research. *Journal of Personality and Social Psychology,* 67(2), 278–286. https://doi.org/10.1037/0022-3514.67.2.278

Matz, S. C., & Gladstone, J. J. (2020). Nice guys finish last: When and why agreeableness is associated with economic hardship. *Journal of Personality and Social Psychology, 118*(3), 545–561. https://doi.org/10.1037/pspp0000220

McCrae, R. R. (1987). Creativity, divergent thinking, and openness to experience. *Journal of Personality and Social Psychology, 52*(6), 1258–1265. https://doi.org/10.1037/0022-3514.52.6.1258

McCrae, R. R., & Costa, P. T. (1985a). Updating Norman's "adequacy taxonomy": Intelligence and personality dimensions in natural language and in questionnaires. *Journal of Personality and Social Psychology, 49*(3), 710–721. https://doi.org/10.1037/0022-3514.49.3.710

McCrae, R. R., & Costa, P. T., Jr. (1985b). Comparison of EPI and psychoticism scales with measures of the five-factor model of personality. *Personality and Individual Differences, 6*(5), 587–597. https://doi.org/10.1016/0191-8869(85)90008-X

McCrae, R. R., & Costa, P. T. (1987). Validation of the five-factor model of personality across instruments and observers. *Journal of Personality and Social Psychology, 52*(1), 81–90. https://doi.org/10.1037/0022-3514.52.1.81

McCrae, R. R., & Terracciano, A. (2005). Universal features of personality traits from the observer's perspective: Data from 50 cultures. *Journal of Personality and Social Psychology, 88*(3), 547–561. https://doi.org/10.1037/0022-3514.88.3.547

Miller, J. D., Lynam, D., Zimmerman, R. S., Logan, T. K., Leukefeld, C., & Clayton, R. (2004). The utility of the five factor model in understanding risky sexual behavior. *Personality and Individual Differences, 36*(7), 1611–1626. https://doi.org/10.1016/j.paid.2003.06.009

Mondak, J. J., & Halperin, K. D. (2008). A framework for the study of personality and political behaviour. *British Journal of Political Science*, *23*, 443–455. https://doi.org/10.1038/s41593-020-0600-3

Norman, W. T. (1963). Toward an adequate taxonomy of personality attributes: Replicated factor structure in peer nomination personality ratings. *The Journal of Abnormal and Social Psychology*, *66*(6), 574–583. https://doi.org/10.1037/h0040291

Onraet, E., Van Hiel, A., Roets, A., & Cornelis, I. (2011). The closed mind: 'Experience' and 'cognition' aspects of openness to experience and need for closure as psychological bases for right-wing attitudes. *European Journal of Personality*, *25*(3), 184–197. https://doi.org/10.1002/per.775

Parker, J. F., & Carranza, L. E. (1989). Eyewitness testimony of children in target-present and target-absent lineups. *Law and Human Behavior*, *13*(2), 133–149. https://doi.org/10.1007/BF01055920

Parkes, K. R., & Razavi, T. D. (2004). Personality and attitudinal variables as predictors of voluntary union membership. *Personality and Individual Differences*, *37*(2), 333–347. https://doi.org/10.1016/j.paid.2003.09.007

Parker, G., & Brotchie, H. (2010). Gender differences in depression. *International Review of Psychiatry*, *22*(5), 429–436. https://doi.org/10.3109/0954026 1.2010.492391

Paunonen, S. V. (2003). Big five factors of personality and replicated predictions of behavior. *Journal of Personality and Social Psychology*, *84*(2), 411–424. https://doi.org/10.1037/0022-3514.84.2.411

Paunonen, S. V., Haddock, G., Forsterling, F., & Keinonen, M. (2003). Broad versus narrow personality measures and the prediction of behaviour across cultures. *European Journal of Personality*, *17*(6), 413–433. https://doi.org/10.1002/per.496

Roberts, B. W., Walton, K. E., & Viechtbauer, W. (2006). Patterns of mean-level change in personality traits across the life course: A meta-analysis of longitudinal studies. *Psychological Bulletin*, *132*(1), 1–25. https://doi.org/10.1037/0033-2909.132.1.1

Robinson, M. D., Moeller, S. K., & Ode, S. (2010). Extraversion and reward-related processing: Probing incentive motivation in affective priming tasks. *Emotion*, *10*(5), 615–626. https://doi.org/10.1037/a0019173

Salgado, J. F. (2002). The big five personality dimensions and counterproductive behaviors. *International Journal of Selection and Assessment*, *10*(1–2), 117–125. https://doi.org/10.1111/1468-2389.00198

Saucier, G., Georgiades, S., Tsaousis, I., & Goldberg, L. R. (2005). The factor structure of Greek personality adjectives. *Journal of Personality and Social Psychology, 88*(5), 856–875. https://doi.org/10.1037/0022-3514.88.5.856

Saucier, G., & Goldberg, L. R. (1996). Evidence for the big five in analyses of familiar English personality adjectives. *European Journal of Personality, 10*(1), 61–77. https://doi.org/10.1002/(SICI)1099-0984(199603)10:1%3C61:: AID-PER246%3E3.0.CO;2-D

Saucier, G., & Goldberg, L. R. (2003). The structure of personality attributes. In M. Barrick & A. M. Ryan (Eds.), *Personality and work* (pp. 1–29). Jossey-Bass-Pfeiffer. http://pages.uoregon.edu/gsaucier/Saucier.Golberg.Structure. Personality.Attributes.P ersonality-Work.2003.pdf.

Schultz, D. P., & Schultz, S. E. (2005). *Theories of personality* (8th ed.).

Schwaba, T., Luhmann, M., Denissen, J. J. A., Chung, J. M., & Bleidorn, W. (2018). Openness to experience and culture-openness transactions across the lifespan. *Journal of Personality and Social Psychology, 115*(1), 118–136. https://doi.org/10.1037/pspp0000150

Shiner, R. L., & DeYoung, C. G. (2013). The structure of temperament and personality traits: A developmental perspective. In P. Zelazo (Ed.), *Oxford handbook of developmental psychology*. Oxford University Press.

Silverthorne, C. (2001). Leadership effectiveness and personality: A cross cultural evaluation. *Personality and Individual Differences, 30*(2), 303–309. https://doi.org/10.1016/S0191-8869(00)00047-7

Silvia, P. J., Nusbaum, E. C., Berg, C., Martin, C., & O'Connor, A. (2009). Openness to experience, plasticity, and creativity: Exploring lower-order, high-order, and interactive effects. *Journal of Research in Personality, 43*(6), 1087–1090. https://doi.org/10.1016/j.jrp.2009.04.015

Soto, C. J., & John, O. P. (2009). Ten facet scales for the big five inventory: Convergence with NEO PI-R facets, self-peer agreement, and discriminant validity. *Journal of Research in Personality, 43*(1), 84–90. https://doi. org/10.1016/j.jrp.2008.10.002

Tellegen, A., Lykken, D. T., Bouchard, T. J., Wilcox, K. J., Segal, N. L., & Rich, S. (1988). Personality similarity in twins reared apart and together. *Journal of Personality and Social Psychology, 54*(6), 1031–1039. https://doi. org/10.1037/0022-3514.54.6.1031

Trobst, K. K., Herbst, J. H., Masters, H. L., III, & Costa, P. T., Jr. (2002). Personality pathways to unsafe sex: Personality, condom use, and HIV risk behaviors. *Journal of Research in Personality, 36*(2), 117–133. https://doi. org/10.1006/jrpe.2001.2334

Tucker, J. S., Elliott, M. N., & Klein, D. J. (2006). Social control of health behavior: Associations with conscientiousness and neuroticism. *Personality and Social Psychology Bulletin, 32*(9), 1143–1152. https://doi.org/10.1177/0146167206289728

Vernon, P. A., Villani, V. C., Vickers, L. C., & Harris, J. A. (2008). A behavioral genetic investigation of the dark triad and the big 5. *Personality and Individual Differences, 44*(2), 445–452. https://doi.org/10.1016/j.paid.2007.09.007

Vize, C. E., Lynam, D. R., Lamkin, J., Miller, J. D., & Pardini, D. (2016). Identifying essential features of juvenile psychopathy in the prediction of later antisocial behavior: Is there an additive, synergistic, or curvilinear role for fearless dominance? *Clinical Psychological Science, 4*(3), 572–590. https://doi.org/10.1177/2167702615622384

Walton, K. E., & Roberts, B. W. (2004). On the relationship between substance use and personality traits: Abstainers are not maladjusted. *Journal of Research in Personality, 38*(6), 515–535. https://doi.org/10.1016/j.jrp.2004.01.002

Weisberg, Y. J., De Young, C. G., & Hirsh, J. B. (2011). Gender differences in personality across the ten aspects of the big five. *Frontiers in Psychology, 33*, 1–11. https://doi.org/10.3389/fpsyg.2011.00178

Xu, X., Plaks, J. E., & Peterson, J. B. (2016). From dispositions to goals to ideology: Toward a synthesis of personality and social psychological approaches to political orientation. *Social and Personality Psychology Compass, 10*(5), 267–280. https://doi.org/10.1111/spc3.12248

Ziegler, M., Cengia, A., Mussel, P., & Gerstorf, D. (2015). Openness as a buffer against cognitive decline: The openness-fluid-crystallized-intelligence (OFCI) model applied to late adulthood. *Psychology and Aging, 30*(3), 573–588. https://doi.org/10.1037/a0039493

Zietsch, B. P., Verweij, K. J. H., Bailey, J. M., Wright, M. J., & Martin, N. G. (2010). Genetic and environmental influences on risky sexual behaviour and its relationship with personality. *Behavior Genetics, 40*(1), 12–21. https://doi.org/10.1007/s10519-009-9300-1

Zhiyan, T., & Singer, J. L. (1997). Daydreaming styles, emotionality and the big five personality dimensions. *Imagination, Cognition and Personality, 16*(4), 399–414. https://doi.org/10.2190/ATEH-96EV-EXYX-2ADB

# 3

# Traits and Biology

**Abstract**  This chapter examines the evidence supporting the existence of a biological foundation for the Big Five personality traits. Early research studies on biological explanations for personality was conducted by Hans Eysenck and Jeffrey Gray. More recently, Colin DeYoung and his colleagues have demonstrated neuropsychological differences that correspond with differences in the Big Five on personality questionnaires.

**Keywords**  Personality • Trait theory • Big Five • Openness • Conscientiousness • Extraversion • Agreeableness • Neuroticism • Heritability • Personality neuroscience

An exciting field of research called personality neuroscience has recently developed to understand relationships between personality, brain anatomy, and neurotransmitters. Different researchers have different theories about how personality and biology are tied together and findings are complex and rapidly changing, though important steps have recently been taken by Colin DeYoung. He suggests that the vast amount of research on the biology of personality can be organized around the Big

Five personality traits. DeYoung (2010) recruited 116 participants to complete the NEO PI-R and associated their scores with differences in the volume of specific brain regions, illustrating that personality differences in the Big Five dimensions correlate with individual differences in brain structure. Additional empirical evidence strongly suggests that the Big Five dimensions of personality have a neurological basis. Furthermore, the Big Five can be traced back to childhood (Shiner & DeYoung, 2013) and are partly heritable (Bouchard, 1994; Bouchard & Loehlin, 2001; Jang et al., 1998; McGue et al., 1993; Larsson et al., 2006; Riemann et al., 1997; Yamagata et al., 2006).

Heritability is the extent to which a characteristic is influenced by genetics and is studied by researchers using family studies, twin studies, and adoption studies. Twin studies often estimate heritability by gauging whether identical twins (monozygotic (MZ) twins), who come from a single fertilized egg (or zygote), thus sharing 100% of their genes, are more similar to each other than dizygotic (DZ) twins, who come from two eggs that were separately fertilized, thus sharing only 50% of their genes like any other siblings. Results reveal that correlations between MZ twins are around twice as large as for DZ twins. For example, according to Bouchard and McGue (1990), the relationship for MZ twins is 0.55 for Extraversion and roughly 0.25 for DZ twins. Similarly, in a sample of 10,000 Swedish twins, Loehlin (1989) found correlations on Neuroticism higher for MZ male twins in comparison to DZ male twins (0.46 vs. 0.21), as well as for MZ female twins compared to DZ female twins (0.54 vs. 0.25). Riemann et al. (1997) examined over a thousand pairs of German and Polish twins to compare MZ and DZ twins on the Big Five. These findings are summarized in Table 3.1.

**Table 3.1** Correlations on the Big Five between MZ and DZ twins (Riemann et al., 1997)

| Domain | MZ twins | DZ twins |
| --- | --- | --- |
| Openness | 0.54 | 0.35 |
| Conscientiousness | 0.54 | 0.18 |
| Extraversion | 0.56 | 0.28 |
| Agreeableness | 0.42 | 0.19 |
| Neuroticism | 0.53 | 0.13 |

The Minnesota Twin Study (Bouchard & McGue, 1990) is the most fascinating of twin-studies, running for 20 years and including extensive testing on 81 MZ twin pairs and 56 DZ twin pairs. Unlike typical twin studies, this study was able to compare the similarity of twins with a shared environment to those raised in different households in order to determine heritability. The results startled many people. Even conservatism calculated at 0.60, which one may have otherwise thought to be heavily determined by an individual's environment. Overall, evidence indicates that identical twins, even if reared in different environments, show greater similarity in personality than other siblings.

Studies of adopted children demonstrate that their personalities bear a greater similarity to the personalities of their biological parents than that of their adoptive parents, even when the children have had no contact with their biological parents. For instance, Loehlin et al. (1985) found children to be more similar to their biological parents than their adoptive parents on various measurements of sociability, including the California Psychological Scale (0.17 vs. 0.04) and Thurstone Temperament Schedule (0.18 vs. 0.02). In summary, research tends to support the notion of personality factors having a sizable heritable component.

## Early Biological Models of Personality

Hans Eysenck's model of personality was one of the earliest to be strongly rooted in biology. Two fundamental personality dimensions of his model were Extraversion and Neuroticism. One of Eysenck's (1967, as cited in Gray & McNaughton, 2003) basic assumptions is that the brain has excitatory (i.e., those that make us alert, aroused, and awake) and inhibitory (i.e., those that make us drowsily, sleepy, and sluggish) mechanisms. He argued that balance between the two produces a level of psychological arousal or inhibition at any given moment, and this balance is regulated by a structure in the brainstem called the ascending reticular activating system (ARAS).

According to Eysenck (1967, as cited in Gray & McNaughton, 2003), the ARAS functions differently for each person, allowing introverts to let in a lot of information while cutting the brain off from stimulation for extraverts. Therefore, a person whose ARAS causes them to be chronically over-aroused is an introvert. As they are already getting lots of sensory input, they avoid stimulation as they already have more than they need. This, therefore, explains why they avoid loud noises and certain social situations, such as noisy parties. A person whose ARAS causes them to be chronically under-aroused, on the other hand, is an extravert. They crave stimulation and seek out sociable situations. In sum, the resting level of ARAS activity is higher for introverts than extraverts.

There is evidence to support the notion that extraverts have a lower level of cortical arousal than introverts do, though not all findings have been replicated. For example, introverts are less tolerant of pain and electric shocks than extraverts (Bartol & Costello, 1976), and have more of an increased heart rate in response to arousing stimulation than extraverts (Richards & Eves, 1991). Furthermore, introverts find it harder to concentrate on tasks when there is noise in the background than extraverts, and typically choose quieter environments to do their work and study (Cassidy & MacDonald, 2007; Dobbs et al., 2011; Furnham & Bradley, 1997; Furnham & Strbac, 2002). Introverts and extraverts also react differently to caffeine, with introverts performing poorer on tasks after caffeine intake, possibly due to overstimulation, and extraverts performing better on certain tasks after caffeine intake, possibly because it stimulates them (Corr et al., 1995). Additionally, PET scans reveal that the frontal lobes of introverts are more active than extraverts (Johnson et al., 1999).

Overall, evidence seems to suggest that Eysenck was about half right; introverts do not appear to be more chronically aroused than extraverts (Stelmack, 1990), and the ARAS does not work like a tap by turning stimulation to the brain on and off (Zuckerman, 1991, as cited in Funder, 2019). However, introverts do seem to react more strongly and often more negatively to sensory stimulation than extraverts (Zuckerman, 1998, as cited in Funder, 2019). In other words, extraverts and introverts are about equally aroused in the absence of external stimulation. However, when loud or bright stimuli are presented, introverts react more quickly and more strongly, and this reaction may lead them to withdraw from certain loud environments.

One of Eysenck's doctoral students, Jeffrey Gray, attempted to improve upon Eysenck's theory by transferring the findings of his early research on animals to humans. Many theorists in this area believe that there is a set of brain structures that cause animals to move towards things they desire or to retreat from things they find frightening. Like Eysenck, Gray (1970 as cited in Gray & McNaughton, 2003) proposed that personality or temperament is based on the interaction of two basic systems in the brain. Gray called these the behavioral approach system (BAS) and the behavioral inhibition system (BIS). The BAS is responsive to incentives, such as cues for reward. When the BAS recognizes a stimulus as potentially rewarding, it triggers approach behavior. The BIS, on the other hand, is responsive to cues for punishment, frustration, and uncertainty.

According to Gray and McNaughton (2003), people differ from each other in the relative sensitivity of their BAS and BIS systems. A person with a reactive BIS is especially sensitive to cues of punishment, frustration, or novelty. According to Gray (1970, as cited in Gray & McNaughton, 2003), the BIS is responsible for anxiety. On the other hand, a person with a reactive BAS is especially sensitive to rewards. According to Gray (1970, as cited in Gray & McNaughton, 2003), the BAS is responsible for impulsivity. Importantly, the BAS and BIS are thought to be independent of one another.

As the BAS is responsible for impulsivity, and the BIS is responsible for anxiety, Gray (1987, as cited in Gray & McNaughton, 2003) has modeled impulsivity and anxiety as an alternative to Eysenck's dimensions of Extraversion and Neuroticism. According to this model, those who are highly extraverted and neurotic are seen as the most impulsive, while those who are introverted and highly neurotic are seen as the most prone to anxiety. Gray and McNaughton (2003) claim that the neurotransmitter dopamine is important for responding to rewards and is an important basis for the BAS. Similarly, low levels of serotonin, a neurotransmitter that helps dampen negative emotions, are thought to be associated with a highly sensitive BIS (Gray & McNaughton, 2003). Low serotonin levels can lead to serious problems. For example, dangerous criminals and people who commit suicide have been found to have low serotonin levels (Mann et al., 1990; Virkkunen et al., 1995). Selective serotonin reuptake inhibitors are a common antidepressant that people take to combat depression.

Recent research has revealed that extraverts develop more neurons that produce and are responsive to dopamine than do introverts (DeYoung, 2010). This might have a genetic basis, but it may come from experience (i.e., those who have a richer history of rewarding experiences may develop more such cells, causing the dopaminergic part of their nervous systems to be well developed and active). Gray and McNaughton (2003) claim that this more active dopaminergic system, or BAS, is why extraverts are more motivated to seek out rewards and are more capable of enjoying them strongly (or at least with more external signs of enthusiasm), as well as why they are more assertive, dominant, and outgoing than introverts. This forms the basis of Depue and Collins' (1999) incentive motivation theory of Extraversion.

Depue's theory states positive emotions are impulses to move towards a desired goal, and that they are responses to incentive rewards and dopaminergic activation (Depue & Collins, 1999). Positive emotions in this context can be compared to Extraversion, or Gray's BAS, as Extraversion is positively predictive of positive affective priming effects (Robinson et al., 2010). Indeed, recently, the relationship between Extraversion and the dopamine system has been well-validated in pharmacological studies, behavior experiments, EEG studies, and neuroimaging research (for reviews, see DeYoung, 2010; Allen & DeYoung, 2016).

# Contemporary Biological Models of Personality

An original idea behind the Big Five is that they are orthogonal, meaning that being higher or lower in one of the traits is not predictive of being higher or lower in another. However, DeYoung (2006) has shown that the five factors are not as orthogonal as originally believed. In fact, there is a small, positive correlation between Conscientiousness, Agreeableness, and Emotional Stability (the reverse of Neuroticism), and there is a small, positive correlation between Openness and Extraversion. In DeYoung's (2006) model, Extraversion and Openness create Plasticity (to explore and engage flexibly with novelty), while Conscientiousness, Emotional

Stability, and Agreeableness create Stability (to maintain stability and avoid disruption in emotional, social, and motivational domains). DeYoung (2010) suggests that these meta-traits may have a biological basis. Specifically, evidence is accumulating to suggest that Plasticity is related to dopamine, while Stability is related to serotonin (Allen & DeYoung, 2016). This is because serotonin facilitates the stabilization of emotion and motivation, as well as the inhibition of aggressiveness and impulsivity, while dopamine facilitates exploration, approach behavior, and flexible cognitive functioning (Shiner & DeYoung, 2013).

There are currently a number of methods available for personality neuroscience outlined by Allen and DeYoung (2016). First, neuroimaging (e.g., magnetic resonance imaging [MRI] or positron emission tomography [PET]) allows for the assessment of brain structure and function with a relatively high spatial resolution. Second, molecular genetics allows for assessment of variation in specific genes that are expressed in the brain. Third, electroencephalograms (EEG) measure the brain's electrical activity at the scalp. Fourth, tests of hormone levels or neurotransmitter metabolites in cerebrospinal fluid. Fifth, the study of the effects drugs have on mood and behavior (i.e., psychopharmacological studies). Personality neuroscience employs these methods in conjunction with the methods of personality psychology (e.g., questionnaires, lab tasks, observations).

As discussed previously, dopamine is an important component in driving behavior in response to potential rewards, as well as any positive feelings that may come with tracking progress towards that goal. Activation of endogenous opioid systems (systems of scattered neurons in the limbic system of the brain) is also consistently associated with pleasant emotions (Nummenmaa & Tuominen, 2018). Therefore, we would expect Extraversion to reflect activation of endogenous opioid systems. Indeed, psychopharmacological studies have demonstrated that endogenous opioid systems responding to cues of affiliation is a function of social closeness, a marker of Extraversion (Allen & DeYoung, 2016). Furthermore, according to Allen and DeYoung's (2016) review, MRI studies have demonstrated that Extraversion is positively associated with brain activity, at rest or in response to positive or rewarding stimuli, in the nucleus accumbens (a part of that brain that aids in the processing of rewards) and striatum (one of the principal components of the basal ganglia, a group of nuclei that are best known for their role in facilitating voluntary movement). Additionally, several MRI studies have found that Extraversion is associated with greater volume of the medial orbitofrontal cortex, a region involved in coding the value of rewards (Allen & DeYoung, 2016).

Openness is conceptually linked to dopamine via Extraversion, curiosity, and novelty seeking. For example, individuals who score high in novelty seeking are more likely to possess dopamine receptor D4 (Matthews & Butler, 2011). Openness is also the only Big Five dimension consistently and positively associated with cognitive abilities such as intelligence, working memory, and latent inhibition, leading Allen and DeYoung (2016) to refer to it as the trait responsible for cognitive exploration. This is not surprising since the aspects of Openness are Intellect and Openness-to-experience, reflecting engagement with abstract or intellectual information and engagement with aesthetic or sensory information. As one would expect, Intellect is more strongly linked to intelligence and working memory than the aspect of Openness-to-experience. An fMRI study found that Intellect, but not Openness-to-experience, was associated with brain activity during a difficult working memory task in two regions of the prefrontal cortex that are involved in the abstract integration of multiple cognitive operations and the monitoring of goal-directed performance (Allen & DeYoung, 2016). This relation remained significant even after controlling for intelligence, suggesting that the regions are involved in intellectual engagement, independent of ability.

As serotonin helps to stabilize information, disrupt impulses, and to focus on goals, it is unsurprising that high serotonin levels have been associated with low Neuroticism (or high Emotional Stability), high Conscientiousness (motivational stability), and high Agreeableness (social stability). Agreeableness has also been closely linked to higher activity levels and volume within several structures of the brain (e.g., left dorsolateral prefrontal cortex, superior temporal sulcus, posterior cingulate cortex; Allen & DeYoung, 2016). Furthermore, high levels of Politeness (an aspect of Agreeableness) are associated with a lower baseline testosterone level (DeYoung et al., 2013; Montoya et al., 2012; Turan et al., 2014). Overall, this combination likely allows for the ability to suppress aggression and regulate emotions.

DeYoung (2010) claims that the neurobiology of Neuroticism highlights a role for the amygdala, given its central role in the BIS and mobilization of negative affect and stress responses. The amygdala is a small structure located near the base of the brain, behind the hypothalamus. It appears to link perceptions and thoughts about the world with their emotional meaning. Research on humans and other animals indicates that the amygdala has important effects on negative emotions, such as anger and fear. When the amygdala is surgically removed from rhesus monkeys, they become less fearful, and sometimes try to eat things that are not edible (Funder, 2019). The amygdala of shy people becomes highly active when they are shown pictures of people that they do not know (Birbaumer et al., 1998), and people with anxiety disorders, who have panic attacks, or post-traumatic stress disorder (PTSD), tend to have an active amygdala all the time, even at rest (Drevets, 1999). Dysfunction in the amygdala, causing lower activation, is related to psychopathy, partly characterized by a lack of anxiety and fear (Glenn & Raine, 2008; Pardini et al. 2014; Yang et al., 2009, 2010, 2012).

## Summary

In sum, according to DeYoung's (2006) model, Plasticity subsumes the Big Five traits of Extraversion and Openness and appears to be associated with dopamine and related brain structures. Stability subsumes Emotional Stability (reverse of Neuroticism), Agreeableness, and Conscientiousness and appears to be associated with serotonin and related brain structures. This work has built upon the models developed by Eysenck and Gray. As illustrated earlier in this text, there is evidence that the five factors of personality emerge early in childhood, are relatively stable, appear across cultures, have neurological correlates, and are partly heritable. The next chapter will now provide an evolutionary basis for the five dimensions of personality.

# Exercises

- Consider the personality traits of three family members in relation to the Big Five. Describe how similar or different each of them is in terms of personality to one another and to you. Think about how genetically close they are to each other and to you (e.g., are they immediate family?) What do you think explains the similarities and differences?

# References

Allen, T. A., & DeYoung, C. G. (2016). Personality neuroscience and the five factor model. In *Oxford handbook of the five factor model* (pp. 1–63). Oxford University Press. https://doi.org/10.1093/oxfordhb/9780199352487.013.26

Bartol, C. R., & Costello, N. (1976). Extraversion as a function of temporal duration of electric shock: An exploratory study. *Perceptual and Motor Skills, 42*, 1174. https://doi.org/10.2466/pms.1976.42.3c.1174

Birbaumer, N., Grodd, W., Diedrich, O., Klose, U., Erb, M., Lotze, M., et al. (1998). fMRI reveals amygdala activation to human faces in social phobics. *Neuroreport, 9*(6), 1223–1226. https://doi.org/10.1097/00001756-19980 4200-00048

Bouchard, T. J., Jr. (1994). Genes, environment, and personality. *Science, 264*(5166), 1700–1701. https://doi.org/10.1126/science.8209250

Bouchard, T. J., Jr., & McGue, M. (1990). Genetic and rearing environmental influences on adult personality: An analysis of adopted twins reared apart. *Journal of Personality, 58*(1), 263–292. https://doi.org/10.1111/j.1467-6494.1990.tb00916.x

Bouchard, T. J., & Loehlin, J. C. (2001). Genes, evolution, and personality. *Behavior Genetics, 31*, 243–273. https://doi.org/10.1023/A:1012294324713

Cassidy, G., & MacDonald, R. A. (2007). The effect of background music and background noise on the task performance of introverts and extraverts. *Psychology of Music, 35*(3), 517–537. https://doi.org/10.1177/030573 5607076444

Corr, P. J., Pickering, A. D., & Gray, J. A. (1995). Sociability/impulsivity and caffeine-induced arousal: Critical flicker/fusion frequency and procedural learning. *Personality and Individual Differences, 18*(6), 713–730. https://doi.org/10.1016/0191-8869(95)00001-M

Depue, R. A., & Collins, P. F. (1999). Neurobiology of the structure of personality: Dopamine, facilitation of incentive motivation, and extraversion. *Behavioral and Brain Sciences, 22*(3), 491–517. https://doi.org/10.1017/S0140525X99372046

DeYoung, C. G. (2006). Higher-order factors of the big five in a multi-informant sample. *Journal of Personality and Social Psychology, 91*(6), 1138–1151. https://doi.org/10.1037/0022-3514.91.6.1138

DeYoung, C. G. (2010). Personality neuroscience and the biology of traits. *Social and Personality Psychology Compass, 4*(12), 1165–1180. https://doi.org/10.1111/j.1751-9004.2010.00327.x

DeYoung, C. G., Weisberg, Y. J., Quilty, L. C., & Peterson, J. B. (2013). Unifying the aspects of the big five, the interpersonal circumplex, and trait affiliation. *Journal of Personality, 81*(5), 465–475. https://doi.org/10.1111/jopy.12020

Dobbs, S., Furnham, A., & McClelland, A. (2011). The effect of background music and noise on the cognitive test performance of introverts and extraverts. *Applied Cognitive Psychology, 25*(2), 307–313. https://doi.org/10.1002/acp.1692

Drevets, W. C. (1999). Prefrontal cortical-amygdalar metabolism in major depression. *Annals of the New York Academy of Sciences, 877*(1), 614–637. https://doi.org/10.1111/j.1749-6632.1999.tb09292.x

Funder, D. C. (2019). *The personality puzzle* (8th ed.). W. W. Norton & Company.

Furnham, A., & Bradley, A. (1997). Music while you work: The differential distraction of background music on the cognitive test performance of introverts and extraverts. *Applied Cognitive Psychology: The Official Journal of the Society for Applied Research in Memory and Cognition, 11*(5), 445–455. https://doi.org/10.1002/(SICI)1099-0720(199710)11:53.0.CO;2-R

Furnham, A., & Strbac, L. (2002). Music is as distracting as noise: The differential distraction of background music and noise on the cognitive test performance of introverts and extraverts. *Ergonomics, 45*(3), 203–217. https://doi.org/10.1080/00140130210121932

Glenn, A. L., & Raine, A. (2008). The neurobiology of psychopathy. *Psychiatric Clinics of North America, 31*(3), 463–475. https://doi.org/10.1016/j.psc.2008.03.004

Gray, J. A., & McNaughton, N. (2003). *The neuropsychology of anxiety: An enquiry into the functions of the septo-hippocampal system* (2nd ed.). Oxford University Press.

Jang, K. L., McCrae, R. R., Angleitner, A., Riemann, R., & Livesley, W. J. (1998). Heritability of facet-level traits in a cross-cultural twin sample: Support for a hierarchical model of personality. *Journal of Personality and Social Psychology, 74*(6), 1556–1565. https://doi.org/10.1037/0022-3514.74.6.1556

Johnson, D. L., Wiebe, J. S., Gold, S. M., Andreasen, N. C., Hichwa, R. D., Watkins, G. L., & Boles Ponto, L. L. (1999). Cerebral blood flow and personality: A positron emission tomography study. *American Journal of Psychiatry, 156*(2), 252–257. https://doi.org/10.1176/ajp.156.2.252

Larsson, H., Andershed, H., & Lichtenstein, P. (2006). A genetic factor explains most of the variation in the psychopathic personality. *Journal of Abnormal Psychology, 115*(2), 221–230. https://doi.org/10.1037/0021-843X.115.2.221

Loehlin, J. C. (1989). Partitioning environmental and genetic contributions to behavioral development. *American Psychologist, 44*(10), 1285–1292. https://doi.org/10.1037/0003-066X.44.10.1285

Loehlin, J. C., Willerman, L., & Horn, J. M. (1985). Personality resemblances in adoptive families when the children are late-adolescent or adult. *Journal of Personality and Social Psychology, 48*(2), 376–392. https://doi.org/10.1037/0022-3514.48.2.376

McGue, M., Bacon, S., & Lykken, D. T. (1993). Personality stability and change in early adulthood: A behavioral genetic analysis. *Developmental Psychology, 29*(1), 96–109. https://doi.org/10.1037/0012-1649.29.1.96

Montoya, E. R., Terburg, D., Bos, P. A., & van Honk, J. (2012). Testosterone, cortisol, and serotonin as key regulators of social aggression: A review and theoretical perspective. *Motivation and Emotion, 36*(1), 65–73. https://doi.org/10.1007/s11031-011-9264-3

Nummenmaa, L., & Tuominen, L. (2018). Opioid system and human emotions. *British Journal of Pharmacology, 175*(14), 2737–2749. https://doi.org/10.1111/bph.13812

Pardini, D. A., Raine, A., Erickson, K., & Loeber, R. (2014). Lower amygdala volume in men is associated with childhood aggression, early psychopathic traits, and future violence. *Biological Psychiatry, 75*(1), 73–80. https://doi.org/10.1016/j.biopsych.2013.04.003

Richards, M., & Eves, F. F. (1991). Personality, temperament and the cardiac defense response. *Personality and Individual Differences, 12*(10), 999–1007. https://doi.org/10.1016/0191-8869(91)90030-F

Riemann, R., Angleitner, A., & Strelau, J. (1997). Genetic and environmental influences on personality: A study of twins reared together using the self-and peer report NEO-FFI scales. *Journal of Personality, 65*(3), 449–475. https://doi.org/10.1111/j.1467-6494.1997.tb00324.x

Robinson, M. D., Moeller, S. K., & Ode, S. (2010). Extraversion and reward-related processing: Probing incentive motivation in affective priming tasks. *Emotion, 10*(5), 615–626. https://doi.org/10.1037/a0019173

Shiner, R. L., & DeYoung, C. G. (2013). The structure of temperament and personality traits: A developmental perspective. In P. Zelazo (Ed.), *Oxford handbook of developmental psychology*. Oxford University Press.

Stelmack, R. M. (1990). Biological bases of extraversion psychophysiological evidence. *Journal of Personality, 58*(1), 293–311. https://doi.org/10.1111/j.1467-6494.1990.tb00917.x

Turan, B., Guo, J., Boggiano, M. M., & Bedgood, D. (2014). Dominant, cold, avoidant, and lonely: Basal testosterone as a biological marker for an interpersonal style. *Journal of Research in Personality, 50*, 84–89. https://doi.org/10.1016/j.jrp.2014.03.008

Virkkunen, M., Goldman, D., Nielsen, D. A., & Linnoila, M. (1995). Low brain serotonin turnover rate (low CSF 5-HIAA) and impulsive violence. *Journal of Psychiatry and Neuroscience, 20*(4), 271–275.

Yamagata, S., Suzuki, A., Ando, J., Ono, Y., Kijima, N., Yoshimura, K., Ostendorf, F., Angleitner, A., Riemann, R., Spinath, F. M., Livesley, W. J., & Jang, K. L. (2006). Is the genetic structure of human personality universal? A cross-cultural twin study from North America, Europe, and Asia. *Journal of Personality and Social Psychology, 90*(6), 987–998. https://doi.org/10.1037/0022-3514.90.6.987

Yang, J., Cao, Z., Xu, X., & Chen, G. (2012). The amygdala is involved in affective priming effect for fearful faces. *Brain and Cognition, 80*(1), 15–22. https://doi.org/10.1016/j.bandc.2012.04.005

Yang, Y., Raine, A., Colletti, P., Toga, A. W., & Narr, K. L. (2010). Morphological alterations in the prefrontal cortex and the amygdala in unsuccessful psychopaths. *Journal of Abnormal Psychology, 119*(3), 546–554. https://doi.org/10.1037/a0019611

Yang, Y., Raine, A., Narr, K. L., Colletti, P., & Toga, A. W. (2009). Localization of deformations within the amygdala in individuals with psychopathy. *Archives of General Psychiatry, 66*(9), 986–994. https://doi.org/10.1001/archgenpsychiatry.2009.110

# 4

# Evolutionary Explanations for Traits

**Abstract** In this chapter, evolutionary arguments are presented that claim to account for the existence of the Big Five personality traits, as well as why there is variation.

**Keywords** Personality • Trait theory • Big Five • Openness • Conscientiousness • Extraversion • Agreeableness • Neuroticism • Evolution, • Animal studies

Darwin's theory of natural selection can be compared to breeding (or artificial selection) in order to better understand the concept. In breeding, humans select particular desirable traits in breeding species. For example, for centuries, humans have selected cows that produce a lot of milk or hens that lay large eggs for breeding, thereby ensuring that their offspring will be more likely to provide humans with a greater quantity of milk and eggs. Natural selection is similar to this, except that nature, rather than people, have selected the traits. It occurs when traits become more or less common in a species because they do or do not lead to greater survivability.

Clearly, if certain traits lead to greater survivability, individuals with those traits will be more likely to produce more offspring than individuals without those traits. Adaptations are inherited solutions to the survival problems posed by hostile forces, such as a preference for fatty foods in order to combat food shortages and a need to belong to groups in order to aid against predators. Intelligence and creativity are also examples of adaptations because they help individuals form solutions to problems of survival.

The evolutionary approach to personality, therefore, assumes that human behavioral patterns developed because they were helpful or necessary for survival at some point in the evolutionary history of the species. For example, aggression has historically helped humans to protect territory and mates, while also leading to dominance in social groups. At other points in history, however, aggression has led to injury and death. Thus, high levels of aggression were useful in promoting human survival during some periods, while low levels of aggression were beneficial during others, explaining the observed variation.

David Buss was the first and most prominent theorist to develop an evolutionary theory of personality. Buss (1991) starts with the assumption that motivation, emotion, and personality are adaptive and argues that the five dimensions of personality can be thought of in terms of solutions to problems of survival and reproduction. Buss' model of personality closely resembles the Big Five, though he uses slightly different terminology. His view is that the following behavioral traits have adaptive significance: Openness/Intellect, Conscientiousness, Surgency (i.e., a disposition to experience positive emotional states, as well as to be sociable and self-confident), Agreeableness, and Emotional Stability.

While Buss was the first to formally propose a complete evolutionary theory of personality, others have followed and made advances to the theory. For example, using factor analysis, Daniel Nettle (2006) proposed a list of costs and benefits for each of the Big Five dimensions (see Table 4.1). A benefit of being extraverted includes being more successful at mating, but a cost is an increased risk of physical injury since extraverts are typically more impulsive. High Openness heightens creativity, though costs include having more unusual beliefs and possibly even developing psychosis. High levels of Conscientiousness can lead to one being hard-working

**Table 4.1** Costs and benefits of the Big Five dimensions of personality (Nettle, 2006)

| Domain | Benefits | Costs |
|---|---|---|
| Openness | Creativity | Unusual beliefs; psychosis |
| Conscientiousness | Hardworking; attention to long-term fitness benefits; life expectancy | Obsessionality; rigidity |
| Extraversion | Mating success; social allies | Physical risk; family instability (i.e., more affairs) |
| Agreeableness | Attention to mental states of others; harmonious interpersonal relationships; valued coalitional partner | Subject to social cheating; failure to maximize selfish advantage |
| Neuroticism | Vigilance to dangers; striving and competitiveness | Stress and depression, with interpersonal and health consequences |

and possibly reaping more rewards, but it also heightens the risk of rigid and compulsive behavior. Furthermore, Conscientiousness can be characterized as a willingness to sacrifice the present for the future, but that is clearly only of benefit if one is able to successfully predict the future. In less stable environments, it is sometimes better to live in the moment.

Importantly, evolutionary psychology is not in opposition to other theories. Instead, evolutionary psychology is complementary to these theories. Evolutionary explanations may help account for the development of Extraversion (or a behavioral approach system, as outlined by Gray) and Neuroticism (or a behavioral inhibition system). As discussed, when mentioning DeYoung's research, Openness can be characterized in terms of an exploratory system, responsible for curiosity and developing new ideas. Agreeableness may originate from a maternal instinct to care for and cooperate with others. Industriousness, a facet of Conscientiousness, is linked to a diligent nature, while Orderliness, another aspect of Conscientiousness, is linked to disgust sensitivity, which is considered an evolutionary adaptation to prevent humans from consuming contaminated foods. Importantly, individuals more easily disgusted by revolting smells and sights are also more easily disgusted by moral transgressions, supporting the notion that these characteristics are reflective of the same underlying construct (see Chap. 10).

It is important to understand that evolutionary arguments do not disregard the significance of environmental factors. In fact, evolutionary psychologists argue that the genetic structure of organisms allows for substantial flexibility in response to their environment (Hibbing et al., 2013, p. 70). They do not claim that personality is solely determined by genetics, but rather that while individuals may have innate predispositions, these can be influenced or modified by their experiences. Another common misconception is that evolution is a conscious and flawless process. Evolution is an ongoing process, and one that includes a lag between adaptation and environmental changes. For instance, if a herd of zebras lives in an area without predators, the genes that influence their speed are likely to remain relatively constant from one generation to the next. But if the herd encounters a new group of predators, the slower zebras are more likely to be targeted, resulting in the faster zebras surviving longer and producing more offspring. This will increase the proportion of alleles that lead to faster zebras over time. Although these changes may not be immediately noticeable from one generation to another, they will eventually accumulate and alter the genetics of the entire zebra population.

The fact that temperament is expressed before and immediately after birth suggests it develops mostly from biological systems but is modified by input from the environment (Gonzalez et al., 1994). For example, some babies are more active than others, just as they differ in sensitivity to sensory stimulation. Temperament differences over the first year of life can even be predicted before birth; a high heart rate at 36 weeks' gestation foreshadows less predictable eating and sleeping habits three and six months after birth (DiPietro et al., 1996). After birth, new-born infants display consistent differences in behavior, especially in terms of activity, emotionality, impulsivity, and sociability (Schultz & Schultz, 2005). Specifically, newborns show evidence of distress and avoidant movements, including anger and frustration, and display individual differences in terms of behavioral inhibition by six or seven months (Rothbart, 2007). Similarly, by two or three months, there are evident differences in approach reactions, measured by displays of positive emotion and body movements (Rothbart, 2007). As children get older, these differences become more pronounced (Schultz & Schultz, 2005). Temperament assessed in infancy can allow researchers to predict a number of later life outcomes, such as teen substance abuse (Tarter, 2002), as well as a number of emotional problems or behavioral problems in childhood (Guerin et al., 1997; Zhou et al., 2009).

In a number of studies by Jerome Kagan, the role of underlying biology has been further supported, as well as the stability and predictive nature of temperament. In one longitudinal study, for instance, Kagan (1997) demonstrated the stability of temperament, as four-month-olds classed as highly reactive were more likely than others to be classed as fearful during middle childhood. Indeed, none of the highly reactive infants could be classed as fearless in childhood, compared to others. However, not all of the highly reactive infants grew up to be fearful children, suggesting temperament is more of a predisposing factor, rather than a determining one. In another study, children rated as being inhibited at three years old scored significantly lower on scales of impulsivity than other children at the age of 18 years (Caspi & Silva, 1995).

Support for the evolutionary basis of human personality also comes from research on animal personality. Most people who have ever owned pets know that animals each have their own unique personalities. For example, some dogs are more aggressive than others. Until the 1990s, most psychologists would have argued that the term personality made sense only as applied to humans, but since then numerous studies have supported the notion that nonhuman animals not only have distinct personalities, but they have personalities on dimensions similar to the Big Five. For example, Gosling and John (1999) conducted a meta-analysis of 19 studies across 12 nonhuman species, finding evidence for at least 14 nonhuman species with personality traits that can be categorized along dimensions similar to the Big Five. A summary of their findings is presented in Table 4.2.

Attempting to apply human characteristics to animals poses some obvious challenges. Nevertheless, the fact that some personality traits, such as Extraversion (behavioral activation), Neuroticism (behavioral avoidance), and Agreeableness (low levels of aggression), are observed in multiple species should not come as a surprise, as they reflect basic survival strategies in animals. Gosling and John (1999) suggest that these traits are characteristic of species that are evolutionarily less advanced. On the other hand, personality traits like Openness and Conscientiousness

**Table 4.2** Table of personality dimensions across species (Gosling & John, 1999)

| Species | Openness | Conscientiousness | Extraversion | Agreeableness | Neuroticism |
|---|---|---|---|---|---|
| Chimpanzee | ✓ | ✓ | ✓ | ✓ | ✓ |
| Horse | | ✓ | ✓ | ✓ | ✓ |
| Rhesus monkey | ✓ | | ✓ | ✓ | ✓ |
| Gorilla | | | ✓ | ✓ | ✓ |
| Dog | ✓ | | ✓ | ✓ | ✓ |
| Cat | ✓ | | ✓ | ✓ | ✓ |
| Hyena | ✓ | | | ✓ | ✓ |
| Pig | ✓ | | ✓ | ✓ | ✓ |
| Vervet monkey | | | ✓ | ✓ | |
| Donkey | ✓ | | | ✓ | |
| Rat | | | ✓ | | ✓ |
| Guppy (fish) | | | ✓ | | ✓ |
| Octopus | | | | | ✓ |

seem to be more reflective of higher stages in evolutionary development and are observed less frequently in various species. Conscientiousness, for instance, typically requires the ability to control impulses, understand values, and organize activities, which may be beyond the cognitive abilities of some animals. Nevertheless, personality traits are evolved solutions that are found in all animals, albeit in different forms. Of course, the more similar the species, the more similar the system, and this is the case also for personality. For example, the personality structure of primates is more similar to that of other primates than it is to that of mammals in general, which in turn is more similar to that of birds or invertebrates. This evidence supports the idea that personality traits evolved millions of years ago, long before modern humans, and have their origins in a common ancestor.

Of course, evolution is constantly occurring, and so there will continue to always be variation, and this too is crucial for the survival of a species. When the bubonic plague swept through Europe in the 1300s and killed half the population, it did not annihilate humanity because individuals possess different immune strengths and weaknesses. Therefore, no human is "more evolved" than another. Evolution involves a species adapting to its environment, which is constantly changing. As a result, evolution is never-ending and not a final destination. Instead, it is a temporary and lagging response to the environmental realities that existed at a particular time. If the environment shifts once more, evolution will take a different course, so no genetically based predispositions, including personality characteristics, are more or less evolved.

# Summary

Evolutionary psychology refers to the scientific investigation of human behavior and cognition from an evolutionary perspective. Natural selection is the process through which evolution occurs, while sexual selection is responsible for the development of certain traits that are attractive to members of the opposite sex, leading to the production of offspring with those traits. Adaptations are evolved strategies that aid in the resolution of critical survival and/or reproductive problems. As products of natural or sexual selection, they must have a genetic or inherited basis. Buss' personality model is similar to the Big Five trait approach of McCrae and Costa, which includes Surgency (extraversion/dominance), Agreeableness, Conscientiousness, Emotional stability, and Openness/Intellect. Buss argues that these behavioral tendencies have adaptive significance. Similarly, Nettle proposed a list of costs and benefits for each of the Big Five dimensions in relation to survivability across the evolutionary history of human beings.

## Exercises

• List several personality traits (lower facets of the Big Five or beyond). Can you think of an evolutionary benefit to each one? If you struggle, consider how they may have helped with survival or sexual selection.

## References

Buss, D. M. (1991). Evolutionary personality psychology. *Annual Review of Psychology, 42*(1), 459–491.

Caspi, A., & Silva, P. A. (1995). Temperamental qualities at age three predict personality traits in young adulthood: Longitudinal evidence from a birth cohort. *Child Development, 66*(2), 486–498. https://doi.org/10.1111/j.1467-8624.1995.tb00885.x

DiPietro, J. A., Hodgson, D. M., Costigan, K. A., & Johnson, T. R. (1996). Fetal antecedents of infant temperament. *Child Development, 67*(5), 2568–2583. https://doi.org/10.1111/j.1467-8624.1996.tb01874.x

Gonzalez, J. J., Hynd, G. W., & Martin, R. P. (1994). Neuropsychology of temperament. In P. D. Vemon (Ed.), *The neuropsychology of individual differences* (pp. 235–256). Academic Press.

Gosling, S. D., & John, O. P. (1999). Personality dimensions in nonhuman animals: A cross-species review. *Current Directions in Psychological Science, 8*(3), 69–75. https://doi.org/10.1111/1467-8721.00017

Guerin, D. W., Gottfried, A. W., & Thomas, C. W. (1997). Difficult temperament and behaviour problems: A longitudinal study from 1.5 to 12 years. *International Journal of Behavioral Development, 21*(1), 71–90. https://doi.org/10.1080/016502597384992

Hibbing, J. R., Smith, K. B., & Alford, J. R. (2013). *Predisposed: Liberals, conservatives, and the biology of political differences.* Routledge. https://doi.org/10.4324/9780203112137

Kagan, J. (1997). Temperament and the reactions to unfamiliarity. *Child Development, 68*(1), 139–143. https://doi.org/10.1111/j.1467-8624.1997.tb01931.x

Nettle, D. (2006). The evolution of personality variation in humans and other animals. *American Psychologist, 61*(6), 622–631. https://doi.org/10.1037/0003-066X.61.6.622

Rothbart, M. K. (2007). Temperament, development, and personality. *Current Directions in Psychological Science, 16*(4), 207–212. https://doi.org/10.1111/j.1467-8721.2007.00505.x

Schultz, D. P., & Schultz, S. E. (2005). *Theories of personality* (8th ed.).

Tarter, R. E. (2002). Etiology of adolescent substance abuse: A developmental perspective. *American Journal on Addictions, 11*(3), 171–191. https://doi.org/10.1080/10550490290087965

Zhou, Q., Lengua, L. J., & Wang, Y. (2009). The relations of temperament reactivity and effortful control to children's adjustment problems in China and the United States. *Developmental Psychology, 45*(3), 724–739. https://doi.org/10.1037/a0013776

# Part II

## Voting Ideologies

# 5

# The Left-Right Debate

**Abstract** This chapter describes the origins of the left-right spectrum in political discourse and provides an overview of how political orientations can be assessed, as well as the true meaning of different political stances. Limitations of using this dichotomy are discussed.

**Keywords** Political orientations • Left-wing • Right-wing

"Left" and "right" have been used for over two centuries to signify the contrast between political ideologies and movements. The terms originated during the French Revolution of 1789, when members of the National Assembly divided into supporters of the monarch to the president's right and supporters of the revolution to his left. They became common phrases and were even adopted by political parties after the Third Republic was established in 1871 (e.g., Republican Left, Center Left, Center Right, Extreme Left, Radical Left). By the early twentieth century, the terms were used to describe the political ideologies of citizens. Those on the left are typically characterized as having political beliefs related to equality, progress, and reform. In contrast, the right is described as representing authority, hierarchy, nationalism, and tradition. Political scientists regard the left as including communists, social democrats, socialists, and social liberals. The right includes conservatives, fascists, imperialists, monarchists, and traditionalists.

There are a number of political movements strongly associated with the left, such as racial equality and trade unionism. However, there are a number of political movements that do not always fit precisely into the left-right spectrum, including feminism; while liberal feminists and conservative feminists often disagree on various issues, such as abortion, there are also common goals related to equal pay and equal opportunities (Renna, 2017). The fight against climate change is often regarded as a movement of the left, but this is also sometimes difficult to categorize in countries such as the United Kingdom. As well as positions on the left and right, there are a number of centrists who are not strongly aligned with either side of the political spectrum.

There are critics who claim that the left-right spectrum is too simplistic. In 2006, British Prime Minister Tony Blair described the main divide in British politics as being open versus closed, as opposed to left versus right (Cowley, 2016). Based upon this model, economic left–right issues are less important than attitudes towards social issues and globalism. Voters described as being "open" are typically more in favor of globalism, multiculturalism, and are socially liberal. On the other hand, "closed" voters are usually conservatives opposed to immigration. This model has gained increasing support during recent years, especially as a result of the 2016 Brexit referendum and 2016 US presidential election, as well as general elections in Poland in 2015 and the Netherlands in 2017. For example, Angela Merkel and Donald Trump are both conservatives, but they clearly fall at opposite ends of the open-closed political spectrum.

In political science, the horseshoe theory is the claim that the far-left and far-right are more similar to each other than either is to the political center. The idea is attributed to French philosopher Jean-Pierre Faye in 1996, though similar ideas existed previously. Proponents of the theory argue that the extremes of the political spectrum both represent a propensity to gravitate towards authoritarianism and totalitarianism. The effect has been used to describe the resurgent hostility towards Jews and new antisemitism from both the far-left and far-right. In recent years, there has been a resurgence of antisemitic attacks, desecration of Jewish symbols, and Holocaust denial. In January 2019, a survey on behalf of the Holocaust Memorial Day Trust found that 5% of UK adults said they did not believe the Holocaust took place. Furthermore, authoritarian type parties on the far-left and far-right mirror each other in significant ways. For example, both the modern Communist Party of the Russian Federation and United States Religious Right strongly support pro-life attitudes and hostility towards LGBT rights. The horseshoe theory, however, has been criticized for oversimplifying political ideologies and ignoring fundamental differences between them. Moreover, even if both the far-left and far-right oppose the same issue, they usually have very different reasons for doing so.

It should be noted that people are generally quite familiar with the language of right and left when asked about their political ideological positioning (Fuchs & Klingemann, 1990). The dichotomy, therefore, helps to simplify the complexity of politics. Studies show that the left-right dichotomy is still employed by citizens when describing their positions on political issues, showing it is still relevant in the political world (Mair, 2007). In many Western European countries, social-economic values remain the most significant in explaining ideological self-placement (Freire, 2006, quoting European Social Survey, 1999). As social issues become more significant to voters, some have argued that political opinions can be better represented by two-dimensional models. In this case, there is typically an economic left-to-right spectrum and a social left-to-right spectrum.

The Nolan Chart and Political Compass are two popular examples of this model, where political opinions are plotted anywhere in a square grid based upon the scores of the two axes. The Political Compass is an online test, designed by a political journalist and a professor of social history. The test consists of 62 propositions the respondent can answer with one of "Strongly agree," "Agree," "Disagree," or "Strongly Disagree." The test-taker falls between −10 and +10 on each axis. The economic left-to-right axis ranges from "Left" (−10) to "Right" (+10), measuring how much or little government intrusion in the economy is favored by the individual. The social left-to-right axis ranges from "Libertarian" (−10) on the far left to "Authoritarian" (+10) on the far right, measuring a person's opinion on government intrusion in personal or social matters.

# Summary

In sum, the left-right dichotomy still has ongoing relevance in the analysis of ideologies. In this model, the left includes ideas to do with equality and progress, while the right contains endorsements of hierarchies and tradition. However, it is important to highlight that it does not always do justice to the diversity and complexity of political beliefs. It is a simplification that tells us something about political beliefs, but certainly not everything.

# Exercises

You may complete the Political Compass here: https://www.political-compass.org/. Consider if your results represent your political views and if you feel the model is a useful method for studying political orientations.

# References

Cowley, J. (2016, November 24). *Tony Blair's unfinished business.* New Statesman. https://www.newstatesman.com/politics/2016/11/tony-blairs-unfinished-business.

Freire, A. (2006). Bringing social identities back in: The social anchors of left-right orientation in Western Europe. *International Political Science Review, 27*(4), 359–378.

Fuchs, D., & Klingemann, H. D. (1990). The left-right schema. In M. K. Jennings & J. W. van Deth (Eds.), *Continuities in political action* (pp. 203–234). De Gruyter.

Holocaust Memorial Day Trust. (2019, January 27). *We release research to mark holocaust memorial day 2019.* Holocaust Memorial Day Trust. https://www.hmd.org.uk/news/we-release-research-to-mark-holocaust-memorial-day-2019/

Mair, P. (2007). *Left–right orientations*. In R. J. Dalton & H.-D. Klingemann (Eds.), *The Oxford handbook of political behavior* (pp. 206–223). Oxford Academic.

Renna, R. (2017). *Political ideology and feelings towards feminism: Why young people reject the feminist label*. [honors capstone projects]. Syracuse University. https://surface.syr.edu/honors_capstone/1026

# 6

# Differences in Moral Foundations

**Abstract** This chapter explores the research conducted by Jonathan Haidt and Jesse Graham, which examines the contrasting moral foundations of liberals and conservatives.

**Keywords** Moral foundations theory • Liberals • Conservatives

Recently, research has examined the different views on morality between voters. When looking at differences between those on the left-right continuum, it is probably not surprising that there would be various interpretations of what is considered moral behavior. Generally, those on the left have taken a more optimistic view of human nature and maintained that people should be as free as possible to pursue their own courses in life. In contrast, those on the right typically argue that people need the constraints of authority and tradition to live civilly with each other. Although moral values vary across cultures, social psychologists have attempted to discern the reasons behind the existence of certain universal norms.

Moral foundations theory, primarily developed by Jonathan Haidt and Jesse Graham, argues that certain moral universals are rooted in intuitive ethics. They claim that there are five distinct universal moral foundations, accounting for the majority of moral decision-making across cultures. Two of these foundations deal with the unjust treatment of others, referred to as the Care and Fairness foundations. The other three foundations focus more on a person's standing with their group, labeled Loyalty, Authority, and Purity.

Research reveals that what people believe are morally right and wrong fairly accurately predicts their political beliefs. Overall, those on the left tend to place greater importance on the Care and Fairness foundations than the other three, whereas those on the right are more likely to emphasize the Loyalty, Authority, and Purity foundations than those on the left (Graham et al., 2009). Therefore, if an individual is being socially ostracized, then a person on the left is likely to view that as morally wrong. However, someone on the right is more likely to ask if the individual is being ostracized because they did something to offend the group. In other words, a person on the right is more likely to wonder and also believe that the individual did something to deserve being ostracized because they typically pay less attention to the hurtfulness of being ostracized and place more importance on group loyalty.

Moral foundations theory might attempt to explain reactions to social protest movements, such as the Black Lives Matter movement. The theory predicts that those on the right may oppose such movements as they consider respect for authority as a moral imperative. Similarly, those on the right are more likely to argue that a soldier should follow orders from a commanding officer, even if the orders seem immoral. In contrast, those on the left are less likely to view Loyalty as being relevant in their assessment of morality, because they are more concerned with Care and Fairness (Graham et al., 2009).

Moral foundations theory highlights that individuals on the left and right have differing emotional responses to their surroundings, which stem from their intuitive moral values. Haidt (2012) employs the metaphor of a rider on an elephant to explain this phenomenon, where the rider represents controlled processes, and the elephant signifies automatic processes. The rider evolves to serve the elephant, indicating that individuals' conscious and rational thought processes are influenced by their automatic, intuitive responses. This is particularly evident when individuals are morally perplexed but still experience strong gut reactions about what is right and wrong, even if they cannot provide coherent justifications for their feelings. This suggests that individuals' moral judgments and emotional responses are deeply ingrained and often operate beneath conscious awareness.

The moral foundations theory also helps explain why those on the left and right differ on issues unrelated to politics. For example, Haidt and Graham asked Americans what sort of dogs they wanted. Liberals were more likely to want dogs that were gentle, while conservatives typically preferred loyal and obedient dogs (Haidt, 2012). Furthermore, when using encephalograms (EEGs) to detect evidence of surprise when individuals were presented with key words, liberal brains showed more surprise, compared to conservative brains, in response to sentences that violated the Care and Fairness foundations, as well as greater surprise to sentences that endorsed Loyalty, Authority, and Purity as moral concerns.

Critics of moral foundations theory argue that the theory is not uncovering new differences, but instead simply reiterating well-known ideological differences. Additionally, they argue that moral foundations theory may wrongly suggest that individuals on the left have a narrower moral sense, when in fact they may simply endorse values that are not included in the theory's five moral foundations. For instance, some critics have suggested that industry and modesty should be included as moral foundations, as they are often moralized in many modern societies (Suhler & Churchland, 2011). Nevertheless, there is strong evidence supporting the cross-cultural validity of the moral foundations theory, as well as reliable differences between individuals' moral foundations based on their political affiliation, particularly in the case of North American liberals and conservatives (Haidt, 2012).

# Summary

Moral foundations theory was developed to explain why morality varies so much, yet similarities and recurring themes still exist across cultures. The theorists argue that there are five innate and universal foundations and that different cultures and societies construct different virtues and narratives on top of these foundations. The five foundations are Care, Fairness, Loyalty, Authority, and Purity. Researchers have found that those on the political right are significantly more likely to endorse the Loyalty, Authority, and Purity foundations than those on the political left across cultures.

# Exercises

You may complete the Moral Foundations Questionnaire here: https://moralfoundations.org/questionnaires/. Consider if your results represent your values and if you feel the model is a useful method for studying differences in morality.

# References

Graham, J., Haidt, J., & Nosek, B. A. (2009). Liberals and conservatives rely on different sets of moral foundations. *Journal of Personality and Social Psychology, 96*, 1029–1046. https://doi.org/10.1037/a0015141

Haidt, J. (2012). *The righteous mind: Why good people are divided by politics and religion*. Pantheon.

Suhler, C. L., & Churchland, P. (2011). Can innate, modular "foundations" explain morality? Challenges for Haidt's moral foundations theory. *Journal of Cognitive Neuroscience, 23*(9), 2103–2116. https://doi.org/10.1162/jocn.2011.21637

# 7

# Genes and Politics

**Abstract** This chapter focuses on the research conducted by Alford, Hibbing, and Smith, which examines the variations in tastes and preferences between liberals and conservatives.

**Keywords** Biopolitics • Liberals • Conservatives

The interdisciplinary study of biology and political science, sometimes referred to as biopolitics, is the application of scientific methods and theories from biology towards the understanding of political behavior. An underlying assumption is that individuals are genetically predisposed to process the environment in a certain way and to prefer particular policies as a result. While some political scientists remain skeptical that political ideologies may be rooted in biology, there have been recent, significant advances in the field. As mentioned in Chap. 3, twin studies have consistently shown that both genetic and environmental factors have an impact on political attitudes (Funk et al., 2013). Even conservatism is highly heritable (Bouchard & McGue, 2003; Bouchard & McGue, 1990). Furthermore, this is a finding that holds across cultures (Bell et al., 2009;

Hatemi et al., 2007). As well as twin studies, molecular genetic studies have confirmed that genes play a role in politics, finding associations between particular genes and certain traits (e.g., Benjamin et al., 2012; Hatemi et al., 2011). Overall, it does seem that genetic factors play some role in shaping political attitudes.

In their 2013 book "Predisposed," Hibbing et al. explored the biological basis of political differences and proposed that genetic differences could explain several variations in tastes and preferences between American liberals and conservatives. To illustrate this idea, the authors used the analogy of beer-loving fruit flies. At the University of California, Riverside (UCR), researchers offered flies a choice between beer and sugar water (Wisotsky et al., 2011). They discovered that some flies had a preference for sugar water and some for beer (due to the presence of glycerol, which is not a sugar but tastes sweet). Afterward, the researchers were able to breed flies that either preferred sugar water or beer, displaying that the variation was at least partly attributable to genetics (Hibbing et al., 2013). Hibbing and colleagues proposed that humans, like fruit flies, exhibit significant variation in tastes and preferences that stem from genetic differences.

Focusing on the different tastes and preferences between liberals and conservatives, Hibbing et al. (2013) pointed out a statement once made by Barack Obama during his primary campaign in Iowa in 2008; "Anybody gone into Whole Foods lately and seen what they charge for arugula?" Obama's opponent, Republican John McCain, meanwhile, professed to not being a big veggie guy, in an attempt to paint himself as an all-American man with a taste for red meat. It may seem silly to think that a presidential candidate would try to connect to voters based upon preferences for food, but in fact, there is strong evidence to support an overall difference in food preferences between liberals and conservatives. In 2009, based on results of 64,000 users who indicated their food preferences and political orientations, Hunch.com found that liberals were more than twice as likely as conservatives to pick arugula as their choice of salad green. The results were then reconfirmed with results of 400,000 further users.

Hibbing and colleagues noted a number of limitations with this research, including that people who used Hunch were not representative of the general population. Therefore, they selected 350 adults at random in a study of their own. They asked respondents, "Given a choice between your favorite meal and a new exotic dish which you've never tried before, which would you choose?" Conservatives were significantly more likely than liberals to choose their favorite meal than the new exotic dish. Conservatives were also more likely to enjoy beef, while liberals were more likely to be vegetarian (Hibbing et al. 2013). There is, therefore, an observable, replicable difference in food preferences between liberals and conservatives.

As well as differences in food preferences, Hibbing et al. (2013) observed a number of other statistically significant differences in terms of likes and tastes between liberals and conservatives. Conservatives preferred their poems to rhyme and fiction that ended with a clear resolution. Liberals were more likely to attend music concerts, as well as to paint and write fiction. Hibbing and colleagues also replicated a finding by Wilson (1990) that conservatives were more likely to dislike jokes that were overtly sexual and that did not provide resolution of incongruous elements. This finding stands across cultures (Hibbing et al., 2013). Conservatives were also more likely to dislike complex representational and abstract artwork (Hibbing et al., 2013; Wilson, 1990). Furthermore, liberals are less likely to have items in their home associated with organization and neatness, such as laundry baskets and calendars, but are more likely to have art supplies, stationary, and to own a broad variety of music (Carney et al., 2008).

Conservatives are also more likely to have strong brand loyalty, whereas liberals are more likely to check for alternatives when doing their shopping (Hibbing et al., 2013). Tierney (2005) has observed a partisan divide in car ownership, noting that Republicans favor Porsches at the high end, while Democrats favor Volvos. On the lower end, Republicans are more likely to prefer American-made cars and Democrats to prefer Hyundais. There are also differences in career paths. For example, academics in the social sciences and humanities are well known for generally being left leaning (Rothman et al., 2005).

Overall, there are a number of observable differences in preferences between those on the left and right of the political spectrum. On the whole, those on the left seem to be more likely to seek out the novel and exotic, while those on the right are generally more loyal to tradition. I would argue that the differences between liberals and conservatives illustrated in this chapter can be largely attributed to variations in personality, specifically the Big Five personality traits. I hope to demonstrate this in the following chapters. As discussed in Chap. 3, personality has a biological basis, with genetics accounting for approximately 50% of the variance in personality traits. (e.g., Bouchard & McGue, 2003). Therefore, this view is not in opposition to the biological arguments of Hibbing et al. (2013) that genetics contribute to political attitudes, but rather complements it with an alternative perspective.

# Summary

Hibbing et al. (2013) observed a number of differences in taste between conservatives and liberals and argued that these differences are partly due to differences in genetic predispositions. We must remember, however, that these differences, while consistent patterns connected to differences in political orientations, are not absolutes. There are differences that exist on average, but these differences are not to be exaggerated. For instance, there are clearly plenty of right-wing voters who are novel writers, and there are obviously left-wing voters who dislike abstract art.

# References

Bell, E., Schermer, J. A., & Vernon, P. A. (2009). The origins of political attitudes and behaviours: An analysis using twins. *Canadian Journal of Political Science/Revue Canadienne de Science Politique, 42*(4), 855–879. https://doi.org/10.1017/S0008423909990060

Benjamin, D. J., Cesarini, D., Van Der Loos, M. J., Dawes, C. T., Koellinger, P. D., Magnusson, P. K., et al. (2012). The genetic architecture of economic and political preferences. *Proceedings of the National Academy of Sciences, 109*(21), 8026–8031. https://doi.org/10.1073/pnas.1120666109

Bouchard, T. J., Jr., & McGue, M. (1990). Genetic and rearing environmental influences on adult personality: An analysis of adopted twins reared apart.

*Journal of Personality, 58*(1), 263–292. https://doi.org/10.1111/j.1467-6494. 1990.tb00916.x

Bouchard, T. J., & McGue, M. (2003). Genetic and environmental influences on human psychological differences. *Developmental Neurobiology, 54*(1), 4–45. https://doi.org/10.1002/neu.10160

Carney, D. R., Jost, J. T., Gosling, S. D., & Potter, J. (2008). The secret lives of liberals and conservatives: Personality profiles, interaction styles, and the things they leave behind. *Political Psychology, 29*(6), 807–840. https://doi. org/10.1111/j.1467-9221.2008.00668.x

Funk, C. L., Smith, K. B., Alford, J. R., Hibbing, M. V., Eaton, N. R., Krueger, R. F., et al. (2013). Genetic and environmental transmission of political orientations. *Political Psychology, 34*(6), 805–819. https://doi.org/10.1111/ j.1467-9221.2012.00915.x

Hatemi, P. K., Gillespie, N. A., Eaves, L. J., Maher, B. S., Webb, B. T., Heath, A. C., et al. (2011). A genome-wide analysis of liberal and conservative political attitudes. *The Journal of Politics, 73*(1), 271–285. https://doi.org/10.1017/ S0022381610001015

Hatemi, P. K., Medland, S. E., Morley, K. I., Heath, A. C., & Martin, N. G. (2007). The genetics of voting: An Australian twin study. *Behavior Genetics, 37*, 435–448. https://doi.org/10.1007/s10519-006-9138-8

Hibbing, J. R., Smith, K. B., & Alford, J. R. (2013). *Predisposed: Liberals, conservatives, and the biology of political differences*. Routledge. https://doi. org/10.4324/9780203112137

Rothman, S., Lichter, S. R., & Nevitte, N. (2005). Politics and professional advancement among college faculty. *The Forum, 3*(1), 1–16. https://doi. org/10.2202/1540-8884.1067

Tierney, J. (2005, April 1). *Your car: Politics on wheels*. The New York Times.

Wilson, G. D. (1990). Ideology and humor preferences. *International Political Science Review, 11*(4), 461–472. https://doi.org/10.1177/019251 219001100404

Wisotsky, Z., Medina, A., Freeman, E., & Dahanukar, A. (2011). Evolutionary differences in food preference rely on Gr64e, a receptor for glycerol. *Nature Neuroscience, 14*(12), 1534–1541. https://doi.org/10.1038/nn.2944

# Part III

Personality & Voting Ideologies

# 8

# The Big Five and Political Orientations

**Abstract** This chapter summarizes the bulk of the research on the association between the Big Five and political orientations. Particularly, there is a consistent finding that those on the left of the political spectrum are higher in Openness, while those on the right end tend to score lower in Openness and higher in Conscientiousness.

**Keywords** Personality • Trait theory • Big Five • Openness • Conscientiousness • Extraversion • Agreeableness • Neuroticism • Political orientations • Left-wing • Right-wing • Liberals • Conservatives • Progressives

Traditionally, income has been used as an indicator of differences in economic attitudes, including views towards issues such as social welfare and increased taxation. Clearly, these attitudes impact voting decisions (Carmines & Stimson, 1980; Rabinowitz & Macdonald, 1989). As seen in Chap. 6, people also often vote in a manner that they feel supports certain moral values they hold, and sometimes they will even do so when it is against their self-interests. This is because both moral foundations and people's circumstances impact voting decisions, as well as many other factors. One of these factors is personality; indeed, like moral foundations, the Big Five personality traits (see Chap. 2) also predict reliable differences in political beliefs across cultures. As a reminder, the Big Five personality traits are:

- Openness (a tendency to be curious and unconventional);
- Conscientiousness (a tendency to be organized and disciplined);
- Extraversion (a tendency to be outgoing and positive);
- Agreeableness (a tendency to be sympathetic and polite);
- Neuroticism (a tendency to be anxious and insecure).

Moreover, there is a significant association between each of the moral foundations and certain Big Five personality traits, supporting the idea that differences in moral standards, political beliefs, and personality traits are closely intertwined. The personality trait Openness is positively associated with the moral foundations of Care and Fairness, while the personality trait Conscientiousness is positively associated with the other three moral foundations (Loyalty, Authority, and Purity). Consequently, those high in Openness seem to oppose constraints on individual expression and freedom, while those high in Conscientiousness are reluctant to violate group-orientated rules (Hibbing et al., 2013).

It has long since been assumed that political orientations are tied to personality, but the Big Five model has more recently given researchers a method to empirically study the association. As explained in Chap. 2, personality is a broad construct that encompasses unique patterns of thoughts, feelings, and behaviors that are expressed through various aspects of our lives, such as our professions, hobbies, home decor, and even the movies we watch. Therefore, it should not be surprising that our personality is also reflected in our political opinions. It is also important to remember that the Big Five model was not designed to find connections between personality traits with politics but is the result of various researchers over the course of several decades identifying clusters of adjectives that tend to go together in describing particular traits, consistently showing the same five categories of descriptions across time and cultures.

A great deal of research has linked these personality dimensions to the differences in tastes and preferences between liberals and conservatives discussed in the previous chapter. For example, those higher in Openness tend to enjoy unconventional music and abstract art. Unsurprisingly, based upon what has been said so far, therefore, those who score high in Openness are also significantly more likely to identify as left-leaning (Carney et al., 2008; Hirsh et al., 2010; Sibley et al., 2012; Xu et al., 2013), and this finding is robust across cultures (Burton et al., 2015; Sibley et al., 2012). Those who score high in Conscientiousness are more likely to be right-leaning, but low Openness is a stronger predictor (Carney et al., 2008; Mondak & Halperin, 2008; Riemann et al., 1993; Trapnell, 1994; Van Hiel et al., 2000, 2004). Therefore, if a person is high in both Openness and Conscientiousness then they are more likely to be progressive than conservative, and if they are low in both Openness and Conscientiousness then they are more likely to be conservative than progressive. Openness and Conscientiousness are the two dimensions of the Big Five most consistently found to be associated with political orientations. These are findings that hold up across time, cultures, and in studies using a wide range of methodological approaches.

One explanation for this association is that individuals adopt ideological positions that provide the best fit with the needs rooted in their psychological dispositions (Jost et al., 2009). In support of this, a study by Block and Block (2006) had nursery teachers score the personality of those in their classes at age 3. Twenty years later, the same participants were asked to report their political orientations in adulthood. Those who were rigid and sensitive to guilt in childhood—indicators of high Conscientiousness—were significantly more likely to self-identify as conservatives in adulthood. Similarly, those who were autonomous and expressive in childhood—indicators of high Openness—were significantly more likely to self-identify as progressives in adulthood. Similar findings have been found in separate, larger-scale longitudinal studies (Fraley et al., 2012). Carney et al. (2008, p. 825) summarizes the findings by saying, "left-wingers are more motivated by creativity, curiosity, and diversity of experience, whereas right-wingers are more motivated by self-control, norm attainment, and rule following."

# Summary

In summary, individuals tend to gravitate towards political orientations that align with the motives and needs rooted in their personality traits. This serves as the basis for the argument put forth in the forthcoming chapters of this text. Particularly, there is a consistent finding that those on the left of the political spectrum are higher in Openness, whereas those on the right are more likely to be low in Openness and/or high in Conscientiousness. The association between political orientations and the other three Big Five dimensions (Extraversion, Agreeableness, and Neuroticism) are less consistent, but will also be discussed.

# References

Block, J., & Block, J. H. (2006). Nursery school personality and political orientation two decades later. *Journal of Research in Personality, 40*(5), 734–749. https://doi.org/10.1016/j.jrp.2005.09.005

Burton, C. M., Plaks, J. E., & Peterson, J. B. (2015). Why do conservatives report being happier than liberals? The contribution of neuroticism. *Journal of Social and Political Psychology, 3*(1), 89–102. https://doi.org/10.5964/jspp.v3i1.117

Carmines, E., & Stimson, J. (1980). The two faces of issue voting. *American Political Science Review, 74*(1), 78–91. https://doi.org/10.2307/1955648

Carney, D. R., Jost, J. T., Gosling, S. D., & Potter, J. (2008). The secret lives of liberals and conservatives: Personality profiles, interaction styles, and the things they leave behind. *Political Psychology, 29*(6), 807–840. https://doi.org/10.1111/j.1467-9221.2008.00668.x

Fraley, R. C., Griffin, B. N., Belsky, J., & Roisman, G. I. (2012). Developmental antecedents of political ideology: A longitudinal investigation from birth to age 18 years. *Psychological Science, 23*(11), 1425–1431. https://psycnet.apa.org/doi/10.1177/0956797612440102

Hibbing, J. R., Smith, K. B., & Alford, J. R. (2013). *Predisposed: Liberals, conservatives, and the biology of political differences.* Routledge. https://doi.org/10.4324/9780203112137

Hirsh, J. B., DeYoung, C. G., Xu, X., & Peterson, J. B. (2010). Compassionate liberals and polite conservatives: Associations of agreeableness with political ideology and moral values. *Personality and Social Psychology Bulletin, 36*(5), 655–664. https://doi.org/10.1177/0146167210366854

Jost, J. T., Federico, C. M., & Napier, J. L. (2009). Political ideology: Its structure, functions, and elective affinities. *Annual Review of Psychology, 60*, 307–337. https://doi.org/10.1146/annurev.psych.60.110707.163600

Mondak, J. J., & Halperin, K. D. (2008). A framework for the study of personality and political behaviour. *British Journal of Political Science, 38*(2), 335–362. https://doi.org/10.1017/S0007123408000173

Rabinowitz, G., & Macdonald, S. (1989). A directional theory of issue voting. *American Political Science Review, 83*(1), 93–121. https://doi.org/10.2307/1956436

Riemann, R., Grubich, C., Hempel, S., Mergl, S., & Richter, M. (1993). Personality and attitudes towards current political topics. *Personality and Individual Differences, 15*(3), 313–321. https://doi.org/10.1016/0191-8869(93)90222-O

Sibley, C. G., Osborne, D., & Duckitt, J. (2012). Personality and political orientation: Meta-analysis and test of a threat-constraint model. *Journal of Research in Personality, 46*(6), 664–677. https://doi.org/10.1016/j.jrp.2012.08.002

Trapnell, P. D. (1994). Openness versus intellect: A lexical left turn. *European Journal of Personality, 8*(4), 273–290. https://doi.org/10.1002/per.2410080405

Van Hiel, A., Kossowska, M., & Mervielde, I. (2000). The relationship between openness to experience and political ideology. *Personality and Individual Differences, 28*(4), 741–751. https://doi.org/10.1016/S0191-8869(99)00135-X

Van Hiel, A., Mervielde, I., & De Fruyt, F. (2004). The relationship between maladaptive personality and right wing ideology. *Personality and Individual Differences, 36*(2), 405–417. https://doi.org/10.1016/S0191-8869(03)00105-3

Van Hiel, A., Pandelaere, M., & Duriez, B. (2004). The impact of need for closure on conservative beliefs and racism: Differential mediation by authoritarian submission and authoritarian dominance. *Personality and Social Psychology Bulletin, 30*(7), 824–837. https://psycnet.apa.org/doi/10.1177/0146167204264333

Xu, X., Mar, R. A., & Peterson, J. B. (2013). Does cultural exposure partially explain the association between personality and political orientation? *Personality and Social Psychology Bulletin, 39*(11), 1497–1517. https://doi.org/10.1177/0146167213499235

# 9

# Openness and Progressiveness

**Abstract** This chapter delves deeper into the finding that those on the left typically score higher in Openness than those on the right of the political spectrum. Explanations for the findings are discussed.

**Keywords** Personality • Trait theory • Big Five • Openness • Left-wing • Liberals • Progressives

Openness is a personality dimension reflected in one's curiosity, preference for art and nature, willingness to try new foods and activities, and ability to re-evaluate one's beliefs (McCrae, 1996; McCrae & Sutin, 2009). Those high in Openness will steer conversations towards talking about ideas, whether it be about philosophy or favorite movies, as opposed to talking about themselves or life events. They "respond positively to unconventional and complex stimuli" (Gerber et al., 2011, p. 269), seek novelty and diversity (Carney et al., 2008), embrace new ideas, and are not rigid (Mondak, 2010). Therefore, it is perhaps not surprising that numerous studies have consistently found Openness to be positively associated with progressiveness and other left-leaning social movements, such as liberalism in North America.[1] A meta-analysis by Sibley et al. (2012) revealed that this association remained robust across various measures of the Big Five (e.g., Big Five Aspect Scales, Big Five Inventory, Costa and McCrae's NEO PI-R, etc.). The study also found that low Openness was the personality trait most strongly associated with political conservatism.

This association holds up using a wide range of political orientation measures. For instance, high Openness predicts decreased right-wing attitudes (Van Hiel et al., 2000; von Collani & Grumm, 2009), less resistance to change (Kandler et al., 2012), lower preference for conservative political parties, and higher preference for North American liberal parties (Hirsh et al., 2010; Mondak & Halperin, 2008). The findings even remain robust when using one-item scales (Carney et al., 2008). Furthermore, these associations reflect differences in actual behavior. For instance, large-sample studies showed that higher Openness predicted individuals voting for the Democrat candidate in the 1996, 2000, 2004, 2008, 2016, and 2020 US presidential elections (Blankenship et al., 2018; Jost et al., 2009, Rentfrow et al., 2009; Xu & Plaks, 2022). A large-scale study in 2012, using samples from two countries (New Zealand and the United States), showed that low Openness was associated with voting for the conservative choice (Osborne & Sibley, 2012). In the UK, high Openness was a large predictor for voting to remain in the Brexit referendum in 2016 (Garretsen et al., 2018). In fact, it was the fourth highest impactor overall, following only education attainment, age, and whether or not one lived in Scotland,[2] even higher than local rates of unemployment or immigration. The finding that those higher in Openness tend to vote for the more left-wing political party also holds up in a number of other European countries (Vecchione et al., 2011). The finding, therefore, remains robust across multiple measures and samples, as well as holds important implications for actual political behaviors.

---

[1] Note: Most of the research has occurred in North America, where liberalism is characterized as being on the left of the political spectrum. However, liberalism may mean something different in other cultures. For example, it is characterized as a more moderate political orientation in the UK.

[2] Note: Scotland voted to remain in the European Union, while the United Kingdom as a whole voted to leave.

Using the facets of Openness in Costa and McCrae's NEO PI-R (see Chap. 2), there is evidence of a strong, positive relationship between American liberalism and the Intellectual Interest facet, which captures one's willingness to entertain novel ideas (Butler, 2000; Carney et al., 2008; Gerber et al., 2011; Trapnell, 1994; but see Van Hiel et al., 2000). This appears to be the facet that researchers focus on most directly when explaining the relationship between left-leaning ideologies and Openness. However, American liberalism has also been consistently found to positively correlate with the other facets of Openness, including Artistic Interest, Exploration, and Tolerance to Ambiguity (Trapnell, 1994; Van Hiel et al., 2000; Van Hiel & Mervielde, 2004). Two facets that have received the least empirical support is Imagination and Emotionality. While some have argued that progressives are typically more imaginative compared to conservatives, not all studies have observed a relationship. Similarly, Emotionality refers to one's feelings of sensitivity, and some have argued that American liberals are more likely to be guided by their feelings than conservatives, but the association between Imagination and Emotionality and liberalism are not as consistently documented in the literature as the other four facets.

As mentioned in Chap. 2, more recent research has found that each of the Big Five personality traits can be empirically divided into two distinct aspects in order to provide more independent predictive power. According to this model, Openness is divided into two aspects: Openness-to-experience and Intellect. The two aspects independently predict separate outcomes. For instance, Intellect predicts general intelligence, as well as verbal and nonverbal intelligence, while Openness-to-experience is only associated with verbal intelligence (DeYoung et al., 2014). Furthermore, Openness-to-experience is positively associated with increased interest in novel stimuli, whereas Intellect is predictive of increased understanding of such stimuli. There have been less studies using this model to test for an association between personality and political orientation, but Hirsh et al. (2010) found an association between liberalism and Openness-to-experience using a sample of 481 community members from Eugene and Springfield, Oregon, and not any independent association between liberalism and Intellect.

As an important characterization of Openness is novelty seeking, and higher endorsement for left-leaning social policies is linked with a stronger preference for complex and unfamiliar experiences (Jost et al., 2003), this may help explain the motivational mechanisms underlying the association. Both being high in Openness and being a progressive can independently be characterized as having a motivation to experience novel information that differs from established norms and both refer to having a preference for creative and original concepts. For example, both Openness and endorsement for progressive politics independently predict wider exposure to media, as well as a preference for media genres classed as more artistic and unconventional, and a dislike for media classed as popular and conventional (Xu et al., 2013; Xu & Peterson, 2017).

Since those high in Openness are open-minded and curious, it has been hypothesized that they are more persuadable (Bakker, 2014). This is because those higher in Openness are typically lower in dogmatism and a need for cognitive closure (Mondak & Halperin, 2008; Onraet et al., 2011). However, research has found no significant relationship between Openness and persuasion, even when that information is tailored towards motivations rooted in Openness (Bakker, 2014). Furthermore, studies have failed to find any support to the notion that Openness underlies a general persuasibility (Bakker, 2014).

In Jungian psychology, introverted intuition and extraverted intuition are the two of the eight cognitive functions associated with scoring higher in Openness (Furnham, 1996; McCrae & Costa, 1989; McDonald et al., 1994). According to this theory, everyone has a dominant cognitive function that they use to make sense of the world, process information, and make decisions (Jung, 2016). The eight cognitive functions are listed in Table 9.1. The Myers-Briggs Type Indicator (MBTI) is a popular assessment instrument, heavily influenced by this work. It tests for eight fundamental preferences and reduces preferences to four scores, meaning that there are 16 possible personality types (see Table 9.2). Each of the 16 types has "a stack" of four cognitive functions, ranging from a dominant

**Table 9.1** Jung's eight cognitive processes

| Cognitive process | Description |
| --- | --- |
| Introverted intuition (Ni) | Forward-looking and focused on the bigger picture, collecting information and sensing patterns subconsciously to make predictions. |
| Extraverted intuition (Ne) | Seeing theoretical possibilities and abstract connections in the environment. |
| Introverted sensing (Si) | Subjective perceptions of the environment and focusing on how those perceptions relate to past experiences. |
| Extraverted sensing (Se) | Responding to that which is tangible in one's environment and that can be detected via the five senses. |
| Introverted thinking (Ti) | Detaching one's self from a situation to study it from different angles and to make it fit with a theory. |
| Extraverted thinking (Te) | Focused on objective data, making decisions based upon logic and measures that can be applied to control external issues. |
| Introverted feeling (Fi) | Paying close attention to subjective feelings in response to a situation, as well as using personal feelings and values to make decisions. |
| Extraverted feeling (Fe) | One's feeling being orientated by one's environment and those around them. |

function to an inferior function, using those defined by Jung. INFJs and INTJs are the two types that have introverted intuition as their dominant cognitive function, and ENFPs and ENTPs are the two types that have extraverted intuition as their dominant cognitive function. Therefore, we would expect these types to score higher in Openness and be more likely to be progressives than other personality types. Indeed, research has found a significant correlation between a preference for Sensing cognitive functions (the opposite to Intuitive cognitive functions) and conservatism and lower political interest, as well as a significant correlation between a preference for Intuitive cognitive functions and identifying as a liberal and greater political interest using multiple samples in North America (Boozer & Forte, 2007).

**Table 9.2** MBTI personality types

| Types | Cognitive function stack | Characteristics |
|---|---|---|
| INTJ | Ni, Te, Fi, Se | Ambitious, logical, self-confident, over analytical. |
| INTP | Ti, Ne, Si, Fe | Ingenious, unconventional, private, insensitive. |
| ENTJ | Te, Ni, Se, Fi | Forceful, efficient, impatient, blunt. |
| ENTP | Ne, Ti, Fe, Si | Adaptive, innovative, mentally quick, procrastinators. |
| INFJ | Ni, Fe, Ti, Se | Insightful, altruistic, determined, perfectionistic. |
| INFP | Fi, Ne, Si, Te | Empathetic, idealistic, impractical, reserved. |
| ENFJ | Fe, Ni, Se, Ti | Charismatic, creative, warm, sensitive. |
| ENFP | Ne, Fi, Te, Si | Curious, friendly, people orientated, flexible. |
| ISTJ | Si, Te, Fi, Ne | Dutiful, responsible, direct, by the book. |
| ISFJ | Si, Fe, Ti, Ne | Patient, supportive, shy, dependable. |
| ESTJ | Te, Si, Ne, Fi | Strong-willed, conventional, loyal, rigid. |
| ESFJ | Fe, Si, Ne, Ti | Sympathetic, organized, value stability, inflexible. |
| ISTP | Ti, Se, Ni, Fe | Practical, spontaneous, stubborn, easily bored. |
| ISFP | Fi, Se, Ni, Te | Charming, passionate, artistic, unpredictable. |
| ESTP | Se, Ti, Fe, Ni | Action oriented, sociable, bold, impatient. |
| ESFP | Se, Fi, Te, Ni | Team player, flexible, dislike long-term plans, relish drama. |

# Summary

Like all left-wing political orientations, progressiveness involves an inclination towards societal change. This would obviously fit into the motivational mechanisms rooted in the personality dimension Openness. Openness, therefore, may predict identifying as a progressive because those higher in this personality trait are more amenable to disruption, including changes in tradition and society. Furthermore, more open individuals are more motivated to seek novel information, which may also help to shape a self-identity that is politically progressive.

# References

Bakker, B. N. (2014). *Personality and politics.* [Doctoral dissertation]. University of Southern Denmark. http://www.sdu.dk/-/media/files/om_sdu/institutter/statskundskab/sidipob/phd+thesis+personality+and+politics.pdf

Blankenship, B. T., Savaş, Ö., Frederick, J. K., & Stewart, A. J. (2018). Piecing together the American voting puzzle: How voters' personalities and judgments of issue importance mattered in the 2016 presidential election. *Analyses of Social Issues and Public Policy, 18*(1), 172–197. https://doi.org/10.1111/asap.12157

Boozer, R. W., & Forte, M. (2007). The relationship of psychological type to political self-perceptions, political opinions, and political party membership. *Journal of Psychological Type, 67*(3), 17–29.

Butler, J. C. (2000). Personality and emotional correlates of right-wing authoritarianism. *Social Behavior and Personality: An International Journal, 28*(1), 1–14. https://doi.org/10.2224/sbp.2000.28.1.1

Carney, D. R., Jost, J. T., Gosling, S. D., & Potter, J. (2008). The secret lives of liberals and conservatives: Personality profiles, interaction styles, and the things they leave behind. *Political Psychology, 29*(6), 807–840. https://doi.org/10.1111/j.1467-9221.2008.00668.x

DeYoung, C. G., Quilty, L. C., Peterson, J. B., & Gray, J. R. (2014). Openness to experience, intellect, and cognitive ability. *Journal of Personality Assessment, 96*(1), 46–52. https://doi.org/10.1080/00223891.2013.806327

Furnham, A. (1996). The big five versus the big four: The relationship between the Myers-Briggs Type Indicator (MBTI) and NEO-PI five factor model of personality. *Personality and Individual Differences, 21*(2), 303–307. https://doi.org/10.1016/0191-8869(96)00033-5

Garretsen, H., Stoker, J. I., Soudis, D., Martin, R. L., & Rentfrow, P. J. (2018). Brexit and the relevance of regional personality traits: More psychological openness could have swung the regional vote. *Cambridge Journal of Regions, Economy and Society, 11*(1), 165–175. https://doi.org/10.1093/cjres/rsx031

Gerber, A. S., Huber, G. A., Doherty, D., & Dowling, C. M. (2011). The big five personality traits in the political arena. *Annual Review of Political Science, 14*, 265–287.

Hirsh, J. B., DeYoung, C. G., Xu, X., & Peterson, J. B. (2010). Compassionate liberals and polite conservatives: Associations of agreeableness with political ideology and moral values. *Personality and Social Psychology Bulletin, 36*(5), 655–664. https://doi.org/10.1177/0146167210366854

Jost, J. T., Glaser, J., Kruglanski, A. W., & Sulloway, F. J. (2003). Political conservatism as motivated social cognition. *Psychological Bulletin, 129*(3), 339–375. https://doi.org/10.1037/0033-2909.129.3.339

Jost, J. T., West, T. V., & Gosling, S. D. (2009). Personality and ideology as determinants of candidate preferences and "Obama conversion" in the 2008 US presidential election. *Du Bois Review: Social Science Research on Race, 6*(1), 103–124. https://doi.org/10.1017/S1742058X09090109

Jung, C. (2016). *Psychological types.* Routledge.

Kandler, C., Bleidorn, W., & Riemann, R. (2012). Left or right? Sources of political orientation: The roles of genetic factors, cultural transmission, assortative mating, and personality. *Journal of Personality and Social Psychology, 102*(3), 633–645. https://doi.org/10.1037/a0025560

McCrae, R. R. (1996). Social consequences of experiential openness. *Psychological Bulletin, 120*(3), 323–337. https://doi.org/10.1037/0033-2909.120.3.323

McCrae, R. R., & Costa, P. T., Jr. (1989). Reinterpreting the Myers-Briggs type indicator from the perspective of the five-factor model of personality. *Journal of Personality, 57*(1), 17–40. https://doi.org/10.1111/j.1467-6494.1989.tb00759.x

McCrae, R. R., & Sutin, A. R. (2009). Openness to experience. In M. R. Leary & R. H. Hoyle (Eds.), *Handbook of individual differences in social behavior* (pp. 257–273). The Guilford Press.

McDonald, D. A., Anderson, P. E., Tsagarakis, C. I., & Holland, J. H. (1994). Examination of the relationship between the Myers-Briggs type indicator and the NEO personality inventory. *Psychological Reports, 74,* 339–344. https://doi.org/10.2466/pr0.1994.74.1.339

Mondak, J. J. (2010). *Personality and the foundations of political behavior.* Cambridge University Press.

Mondak, J. J., & Halperin, K. D. (2008). A framework for the study of personality and political behaviour. *British Journal of Political Science, 38*(2), 335–362. https://doi.org/10.1017/S0007123408000173

Onraet, E., Van Hiel, A., Roets, A., & Cornelis, I. (2011). The closed mind: 'Experience' and 'cognition' aspects of openness to experience and need for closure as psychological bases for right-wing attitudes. *European Journal of Personality, 25*(3), 184–197. https://doi.org/10.1002/per.775

Osborne, D., & Sibley, C. G. (2012). Does personality matter? Openness correlates with vote choice, but particularly for politically sophisticated voters. *Journal of Research in Personality, 46*(6), 743–751. https://doi.org/10.1016/j.jrp.2012.09.001

Rentfrow, P. J., Jost, J. T., Gosling, S. D., & Potter, J. (2009). Statewide differences in personality predict voting patterns in 1996–2004 US presidential elections. *Social and Psychological Bases of Ideology and System Justification, 1,* 314–349.

Sibley, C. G., Osborne, D., & Duckitt, J. (2012). Personality and political orientation: Meta-analysis and test of a threat-constraint model. *Journal of Research in Personality, 46*(6), 664–677. https://doi.org/10.1016/j.jrp.2012.08.002

Trapnell, P. D. (1994). Openness versus intellect: A lexical left turn. *European Journal of Personality, 8*(4), 273–290. https://doi.org/10.1002/per.2410 080405

Van Hiel, A., Kossowska, M., & Mervielde, I. (2000). The relationship between openness to experience and political ideology. *Personality and Individual Differences, 28*(4), 741–751. https://doi.org/10.1016/S0191-8869(99) 00135-X

Van Hiel, A., & Mervielde, I. (2004). Openness to experience and boundaries in the mind: Relationships with cultural and economic conservative beliefs. *Journal of Personality, 72*(4), 659–686. https://doi.org/10.1111/j.0022-3506.2004.00276.x

Vecchione, M., Schoen, H., Castro, J. L. G., Cieciuch, J., Pavlopoulos, V., & Caprara, G. V. (2011). Personality correlates of party preference: The big five in five big European countries. *Personality and Individual Differences, 51*(6), 737–742. https://doi.org/10.1016/j.paid.2011.06.015

von Collani, G., & Grumm, M. (2009). On the dimensional structure of personality, ideological beliefs, social attitudes, and personal values. *Journal of Individual Differences, 30*(2), 107–119. https://doi.org/10.1027/1614-0001.30.2.107

Xu, X., Mar, R. A., & Peterson, J. B. (2013). Does cultural exposure partially explain the association between personality and political orientation? *Personality and Social Psychology Bulletin, 39*(11), 1497–1517. https://doi.org/10.1177/0146167213499235

Xu, X., & Peterson, J. B. (2017). Differences in media preference mediate the link between personality and political orientation. *Political Psychology, 38*(1), 55–72. https://doi.org/10.1111/pops.12307

Xu, X., & Plaks, J. E. (2022). Aspect-level personality characteristics of US presidential candidate supporters in the 2016 and 2020 elections. *Social Psychological and Personality Science, 14*(5), 588. https://doi.org/10.1177/19485506221113954

# 10

# Conscientiousness, Conservatism, and Disgust Sensitivity

**Abstract** This chapter describes research finding that conservatism is associated with Conscientiousness, as well as Dutifulness, Orderliness, and disgust sensitivity. It is argued that these findings align with the research by Haidt and Graham, which suggests that conservatives tend to place greater emphasis on specific moral foundations such as group loyalty, obedience to authority, and purity.

**Keywords** Personality • Trait theory • Big Five • Openness • Conscientiousness • Industrious • Orderliness • Right-wing • Conservatives • Disgust • Behavioral immune system • Pathogen avoidance

Like the association between Openness and progressiveness, a great deal of research has documented a relationship between Conscientiousness and conservatism, using various measures of personality and samples. However, it is important to note that the association is weaker, and that low Openness is a stronger predictor of political conservatism (Sibley et al., 2012). Particularly, the association between Conscientiousness and economic conservatism is less consistent (Gerber et al., 2010, 2011; Leeson & Heaven, 1999; but see Carney et al., 2008; Riemann et al., 1993; Sibley & Duckitt, 2008; Van Hiel & Mervielde, 2004; Gerber et al., 2010, p. 115), compared to Conscientiousness and social conservatism. The relationship between Conscientiousness and social conservatism is perhaps best explained by the fact that conservatism is characterized as a preference to "adhere to social norms and rules" (Gerber et al., 2010, p. 115) and that Dutifulness (a facet of Conscientiousness) captures loyalty and obedience (Costa et al., 1991). This would also explain the connection to several moral foundations, including Loyalty, Authority, and Purity (see Chap. 6). Similarly, looking at the personality model by DeYoung (2006), Orderliness (an aspect of Conscientiousness), conceptually and empirically linked to Dutifulness, is also associated with conservatism (Hirsh et al., 2010).

More recently, a strong association between conservatism and disgust has been unearthed. Disgust is an emotional process, elicited by potentially contaminating stimuli, thought to be an evolutionary specialization to help avoid contact with contaminated foods (Haidt et al., 1994). Individuals who report a higher degree of disgust sensitivity (i.e., the tendency to feel disgust) have been found to hold more conservative political views on a range of topics, including abortion and gay marriage (Inbar et al., 2009). Those who reported a higher level of disgust sensitivity were also more likely to vote for John McCain than Barack Obama in the 2008 elections (Inbar et al., 2012), as well as for Donald Trump in the 2016 elections. In fact, the odds of a participant voting for Trump versus Clinton increased by 30% for every unit increase in sexual disgust sensitivity (i.e., an aversion to short-term sexual relationships; Billingsley et al., 2018).

Importantly, this finding is not restricted to the United States. The association between higher disgust sensitivity and higher conservatism was also revealed in a large-scale study looking at participants in 10 distinct world regions (Inbar et al., 2012). Furthermore, the association between conservatism and disgust is not only evident in self-report measures of disgust sensitivity, but also in stronger neurophysiological reactions to repulsive images during laboratory experiments (Smith et al., 2011). It also does not only apply to disgust towards physical contagions, but also disgust towards social misconducts, such as cheating (Chapman et al., 2009). For example, moral transgressions described as "disgusting" receive higher condemnation from those higher in disgust sensitivity (Chapman & Anderson, 2014; Horberg et al., 2009; Jones & Fitness, 2008; Karinen & Chapman, 2019).[1]

Taking a personality psychology perspective, it is not surprising to see a correlation between disgust sensitivity and political conservatism. Disgust is associated with Orderliness (an aspect of Conscientiousness), and as already discussed, one is able to reliably predict political conservatism via Conscientiousness, particularly Orderliness (Hirsh et al., 2010). If those more easily disgusted tend to be politically conservative, as do those who have a preference for order, it would make sense that these three constructs are interlinked. Indeed, research shows that Orderliness is a consistent mediator of the association between disgust sensitivity and conservatism. Therefore, it seems that more disgust-sensitive people extend their preference for order to the political world (Xu et al., 2020).

One proposed explanation for this association is the motivation to avoid disease (Xu et al., 2020). The debate over opening borders is an age-old political dispute. Ancient cities were built with great walls, and sometimes the right thing to do was to open the gates to receive a wealth of knowledge and resources. Other times, opening the gates killed the entire city as foreigners brought disease and violence. Survival through avoidance is a major evolutionary driving force, as the majority of deaths until a little over a century ago were due to infectious diseases (Volk & Atkinson, 2013). Disgust is a key component of the behavioral immune system, which gives rise to relevant infection avoiding behaviors, such as food preparation, personal hygiene, and avoidance of risky sexual interactions (Oaten et al., 2009). This system is responsible for psychological response mechanisms that pick up on cues to predict the presence of infectious diseases. For example, historically, people with skin lesions were more likely to be carriers of infections than those without, and thus were shunned and persecuted.

---

[1] On a similar note, as jurors, conscientious individuals are more likely to support a harsher punishment if a defendant has been found guilty (Clark et al., 2007).

The behavioral immune system has significant implications for social interactions (Schaller & Park, 2011), as it promotes socially conservative values that seek to avoid contact with out-group members (Xu et al., 2020). One consequence of the behavioral immune system is that as pathogen prevalence increases, so does right-wing attitudes, authoritarianism, and xenophobia. The parasite stress hypothesis posits that behaviors like conformity, ethnocentrism, and distrust of others arise during times of high infection levels to minimize the chances of exposure. This is supported by the fact that, typically, people who feel more vulnerable to disease report higher levels of ethnocentrism and xenophobia (Navarrete & Fessler, 2006).

Together, these findings support arguments made by evolutionary theorists that higher disgust sensitivity leads to greater out-group avoidance and in-group attraction (Faulkner et al., 2004; Navarrette & Fessler, 2006), underlying conservative values (Terrizzi et al., 2013). A meta-analysis of 24 studies further supports the notion that higher disgust sensitivity relates to social conservatism (Terrizzi et al., 2013). Furthermore, recent, cross-national evidence supports this hypothesis in two significant ways. First of all, parasite prevalence strongly predicts cross-national differences in authoritarian personalities and authoritarian governance (i.e., the more pathogens in an area, the more authoritarian views are likely to be held by individuals in the area and the more likely the local government is to be authoritarian). Second of all, this correlation remains statistically significant even when controlling for other threats to human welfare, such as famine and war (Murray et al., 2013).[2]

Out of the two aspects of Conscientiousness, Orderliness predicts political conservatism, but not Industriousness (Hirsh et al., 2010). This association may be due to the fact that high Orderliness is linked to lower tolerance for uncertainty and a greater need for tradition (Jost et al., 2003; Xu et al., 2016), as well as to higher disgust sensitivity (Karinen &

---

[2] Right-Wing Authoritarianism (RWA) will be discussed more in Chap. 12, but it is a socially conservative value system and is characterized by obedience to authority and adherence to tradition (Altemeyer, 1988). Furthermore, it promotes in-group cohesion and intolerance towards out-groups (Haidt et al., 1994). Research reveals that behavioral immune strength, including concerns about cleanliness and feelings of disgust, is linked to both political conservatism and RWA (Terrizzi et al., 2013).

Chapman, 2019). If one is able to keep an orderly environment, and one that fosters familiarity, it will be easier to notice signs of contamination, as well as to reduce exposure to unknown, potentially dangerous stimuli. Orderliness, therefore, contributes to pathogen avoidance (Xu et al., 2020). If this is true, social conservatism may stem from a motivation to mitigate the risks posed by unknown threats. The pathogen-avoidance explanation accounts for three main observations, including that (1) those more easily disgusted are more orderly, (2) those more orderly are more likely to be socially right-wing (or conservative), (3) and those more socially right-wing are more likely to endorse political policies that are in accordance with pathogen avoidance. This model is thought to explain why social conservatism often endorses political policies that support out-group avoidance, as even superficial markers of out-groups, including unfamiliar ethnicities and cultures, may activate the behavioral immune system (Billingsley et al., 2018).

Conservatives have been described by some researchers as having hypervigilant behavioral immune systems (Aarøe et al., 2017). From an evolutionary perspective, this would make sense, as the costs of the behavioral immune system producing a false negative (i.e., failing to detect pathogens that are present) is likely to outweigh costs of a false positive (i.e., incorrectly detecting pathogens that are actually not present; Tybur & Lieberman, 2016, as cited in Billingsley et al., 2018). Therefore, it seems as though disgust encourages one to be orderly, which, in turn, encourages the endorsement of political policies aimed to uphold societal order (Xu et al., 2020). The most impressive evidence for this comes from cross-cultural research showing that regions with higher levels of disease prevalence tend to be associated with higher levels of social conformity and autocratic rule (Murray et al., 2011). For instance, during the COVID-19 pandemic, there was an increase in socially conservative views, especially in regard to conforming more strongly to traditional gender roles and believing more strongly in traditional gender stereotypes (Rosenfeld & Tomiyama, 2021) Furthermore, situational reminders of the importance of physical cleanliness, such as asking participants to wipe their hands with antiseptic wipes, tend to increase self-reported political conservatism (Helzer & Pizarro, 2011). The association between Conscientiousness, conservatism, and disgust, therefore, may be explained by a pathogen-avoidance theory. If roles and rules are unambiguous, violators can be easily detected, thereby helping to keep society as orderly as possible.

Importantly, however, this is a complicated, multifactorial issue. For instance, social conservatism did not predict compliance with pathogen-avoidant policies during the COVID-19 pandemic. In fact, North American conservatives were less likely than liberals to follow social distancing, wear masks, and were less concerned about the pandemic (Gadarian et al., 2021; Kempthorne & Terrizzi, 2021; Xu & Cheng, 2021). This may be because the policies interfered with other concerns, such as lockdowns possibly leading to weaker economies. It may also be due to some of the strategies implemented for dealing with COVID-19. For instance, disgust towards needles and blood promotes anti-vaccination attitudes (Hornsey et al., 2018). Pathogen disgust sensitivity also increases vaccine skepticism and belief that vaccines cause autism (Clifford & Wendell, 2016). Therefore, unsurprisingly, during the COVID-19 pandemic, disgust sensitivity and social conservatism were both positively correlated with anti-vaccination attitudes (Kempthorne & Terrizzi, 2021). Another explanation for these findings is that pathogen avoidant behavior was directed by party loyalty and source of information and media consumption (e.g., Kempthorne & Terrizzi, 2021; Murphy et al., 2021). Indeed, during the COVID-19 pandemic in the United States, social conservatism predicted endorsement of pathogen-avoidant policies amongst Democrats, but not amongst Republicans (Samore et al., 2021).

# Summary

Disgust encourages one to be orderly, which, in turn, may encourage the endorsement of political policies aimed to uphold societal order. Indeed, situational reminders of the importance of physical cleanliness tend to increase self-reported political conservatism and higher levels of disease prevalence tend to be associated with higher levels of social conformity. However, this is a complicated relationship that may be moderated by threats to other values.

# References

Aarøe, L., Petersen, M. B., & Arceneaux, K. (2017). The behavioral immune system shapes political intuitions: Why and how individual differences in disgust sensitivity underlie opposition to immigration. *American Political Science Review, 111*(2), 277–294. https://doi.org/10.1017/S0003055416000770

Altemeyer, B. (1988). *Enemies of freedom: Understanding right-wing authoritarianism.* Jossey-Bass.

Billingsley, J., Lieberman, D., & Tybur, J. M. (2018). Sexual disgust trumps pathogen disgust in predicting voter behavior during the 2016 U.S. Presidential election. *Evolutionary Psychology, 16*(2), 1474704918764170. https://doi.org/10.1177/1474704918764170

Carney, D. R., Jost, J. T., Gosling, S. D., & Potter, J. (2008). The secret lives of liberals and conservatives: Personality profiles, interaction styles, and the things they leave behind. *Political Psychology, 29*(6), 807–840. https://doi.org/10.1111/j.1467-9221.2008.00668.x

Chapman, H. A., & Anderson, A. K. (2014). Trait physical disgust is related to moral judgments outside of the purity domain. *Emotion, 14*(2), 341–348. https://doi.org/10.1037/a0035120

Chapman, H. A., Kim, D. A., Susskind, J. M., & Anderson, A. K. (2009). In bad taste: Evidence for the oral origins of moral disgust. *Science, 323*(5918), 1222–1226. https://doi.org/10.1126/science.1165565

Clark, J., Boccaccini, M. T., Caillouet, B., & Chaplin, W. F. (2007). Five factor model personality traits, jury selection, and case outcomes in criminal and civil cases. *Criminal Justice and Behavior, 34*(5), 641–660. https://doi.org/10.1177/0093854806297555

Clifford, S., & Wendell, D. G. (2016). How disgust influences health purity attitudes. *Political Behavior, 38*(1), 155–178. https://doi.org/10.1007/s11109-015-9310-z

Costa, P. T., Jr., McCrae, R. R., & Dye, D. A. (1991). Facet scales for agreeableness and conscientiousness: A revision of the NEO personality inventory. *Personality and Individual Differences, 12*(9), 887–898. https://doi.org/10.1016/0191-8869(91)90177-D

DeYoung, C. G. (2006). Higher-order factors of the big five in a multi-informant sample. *Journal of Personality and Social Psychology, 91*(6), 1138–1151. https://doi.org/10.1037/0022-3514.91.6.1138

Faulkner, J., Schaller, M., Park, J. H., & Duncan, L. A. (2004). Evolved disease-avoidance mechanisms and contemporary xenophobic attitudes. *Group Processes & Intergroup Relations, 7*(4), 333–353. https://doi.org/10.1177/1368430204046142

Gadarian, S. K., Goodman, S. W., & Pepinsky, T. B. (2021). Partisanship, health behavior, and policy attitudes in the early stages of the COVID-19 pandemic. *PLoS One, 16*(4), e0249596. https://doi.org/10.1371/journal.pone.0249596

Gerber, A. S., Huber, G. A., Doherty, D., Dowling, C. M., & Ha, S. E. (2010). Personality and political attitudes: Relationships across issue domains and political contexts. *American Political Science Review, 104*(1), 111–133. https://doi.org/10.1017/S0003055410000031

Gerber, A. S., Huber, G. A., Doherty, D., & Dowling, C. M. (2011). The big five personality traits in the political arena. *Annual Review of Political Science, 14*, 265–287.

Haidt, J., McCauley, C., & Rozin, P. (1994). Individual differences in sensitivity to disgust: A scale sampling seven domains of disgust elicitors. *Personality and Individual Differences, 16*(5), 701–713. https://doi.org/10.1016/0191-8869(94)90212-7

Helzer, E. G., & Pizarro, D. A. (2011). Dirty liberals! Reminders of physical cleanliness influence moral and political attitudes. *Psychological Science, 22*(4), 517–522. https://doi.org/10.1177/0956797611402514

Hirsh, J. B., DeYoung, C. G., Xu, X., & Peterson, J. B. (2010). Compassionate liberals and polite conservatives: Associations of agreeableness with political ideology and moral values. *Personality and Social Psychology Bulletin, 36*(5), 655–664. https://doi.org/10.1177/0146167210366854

Horberg, E. J., Oveis, C., Keltner, D., & Cohen, A. B. (2009). Disgust and the moralization of purity. *Journal of Personality and Social Psychology, 97*(6), 963–976. https://doi.org/10.1037/a0017423

Hornsey, M. J., Harris, E. A., & Fielding, K. S. (2018). The psychological roots of anti-vaccination attitudes: A 24-nation investigation. *Health Psychology, 37*(4), 307–315. https://doi.org/10.1037/hea0000586

Inbar, Y., Pizarro, D. A., & Bloom, P. (2009). Conservatives are more easily disgusted than liberals. *Cognition and Emotion, 23*(4), 714–725. https://doi.org/10.1080/02699930802110007

Inbar, Y., Pizarro, D., Iyer, R., & Haidt, J. (2012). Disgust sensitivity, political conservatism, and voting. *Social Psychological and Personality Science, 3*(5), 537–544. https://doi.org/10.1177/1948550611429024

Jones, A., & Fitness, J. (2008). Moral hypervigilance: The influence of disgust sensitivity in the moral domain. *Emotion, 8*(5), 613–627. https://doi.org/10.1037/a0013435

Jost, J. T., Glaser, J., Kruglanski, A. W., & Sulloway, F. J. (2003). Political conservatism as motivated social cognition. *Psychological Bulletin, 129*(3), 339–375. https://doi.org/10.1037/0033-2909.129.3.339

Karinen, A. K., & Chapman, H. A. (2019). Cognitive and personality correlates of trait disgust and their relationship to condemnation of nonpurity moral transgressions. *Emotion, 19*(5), 889–902. https://doi.org/10.1037/emo0000489

Kempthorne, J. C., & Terrizzi, J. A., Jr. (2021). The behavioral immune system and conservatism as predictors of disease-avoidant attitudes during the COVID-19 pandemic. *Personality and Individual Differences, 178*, 110857. https://doi.org/10.1016/j.paid.2021.110857

Leeson, P., & Heaven, P. C. (1999). Social attitudes and personality. *Australian Journal of Psychology, 51*(1), 19–24. https://doi.org/10.1080/00049539908255330

Murphy, J., Vallières, F., Bentall, R. P., Shevlin, M., McBride, O., Hartman, T. K., et al. (2021). Psychological characteristics associated with COVID-19 vaccine hesitancy and resistance in Ireland and the United Kingdom. *Nature Communications, 12*(1), 29. https://doi.org/10.1038/s41467-020-20226-9

Murray, D. R., Schaller, M., & Suedfeld, P. (2013). Pathogens and politics: Further evidence that parasite prevalence predicts authoritarianism. *PloS One, 8*(5), e62275. https://doi.org/10.1371/journal.pone.0062275

Murray, D. R., Trudeau, R., & Schaller, M. (2011). On the origins of cultural differences in conformity: Four tests of the pathogen prevalence hypothesis. *Personality and Social Psychology Bulletin, 37*(3), 318–329. https://doi.org/10.1177/0146167210394451

Navarrete, C. D., & Fessler, D. M. (2006). Disease avoidance and ethnocentrism: The effects of disease vulnerability and disgust sensitivity on intergroup attitudes. *Evolution and Human Behavior, 27*(4), 270–282. https://doi.org/10.1016/j.evolhumbehav.2005.12.001

Oaten, M., Stevenson, R. J., & Case, T. I. (2009). Disgust as a disease-avoidance mechanism. *Psychological Bulletin, 135*(2), 303–321. https://doi.org/10.1037/a0014823

Riemann, R., Grubich, C., Hempel, S., Mergl, S., & Richter, M. (1993). Personality and attitudes towards current political topics. *Personality and Individual Differences, 15*(3), 313–321. https://doi.org/10.1016/0191-8869(93)90222-O

Rosenfeld, D. L., & Tomiyama, A. J. (2021). Can a pandemic make people more socially conservative? Political ideology, gender roles, and the case of COVID-19. *Journal of Applied Social Psychology, 51*(4), 425–433. https://doi.org/10.1111/jasp.12745

Samore, T., Fessler, D. M., Sparks, A. M., & Holbrook, C. (2021). Of pathogens and party lines: Social conservatism positively associates with COVID-19 precautions among US democrats but not republicans. *PLoS One, 16*(6), e0253326. https://doi.org/10.1371/journal.pone.0253326

Schaller, M., & Park, J. H. (2011). The behavioral immune system (and why it matters). *Current Directions in Psychological Science, 20*(2), 99–103. https://doi.org/10.1177/0963721411402596

Sibley, C. G., & Duckitt, J. (2008). Personality and prejudice: A meta-analysis and theoretical review. *Personality and Social Psychology Review, 12*(3), 248–279. https://doi.org/10.1177/1088868308319226

Sibley, C. G., Osborne, D., & Duckitt, J. (2012). Personality and political orientation: Meta-analysis and test of a threat-constraint model. *Journal of Research in Personality, 46*(6), 664–677. https://doi.org/10.1016/j.jrp.2012.08.002

Smith, K. B., Oxley, D., Hibbing, M. V., Alford, J. R., & Hibbing, J. R. (2011). Disgust sensitivity and the neurophysiology of left-right political orientations. *PLoS One, 6*(10), e25552. https://doi.org/10.1371/journal.pone.0025552

Terrizzi, J. A., Jr., Shook, N. J., & McDaniel, M. A. (2013). The behavioral immune system and social conservatism: A meta-analysis. *Evolution and Human Behavior, 34*(2), 99–108. https://doi.org/10.1016/j.evolhumbehav.2012.10.003

Van Hiel, A., & Mervielde, I. (2004). Openness to experience and boundaries in the mind: Relationships with cultural and economic conservative beliefs. *Journal of Personality, 72*(4), 659–686. https://doi.org/10.1111/j.0022-3506.2004.00276.x

Volk, A. A., & Atkinson, J. A. (2013). Infant and child death in the human environment of evolutionary adaptation. *Evolution and Human Behavior, 34*(3), 182–192. https://doi.org/10.1016/j.evolhumbehav.2012.11.007

Xu, P., & Cheng, J. (2021). Individual differences in social distancing and mask-wearing in the pandemic of COVID-19: The role of need for cognition, self-control and risk attitude. *Personality and Individual Differences, 175*, 110706. https://doi.org/10.1016/j.paid.2021.110706

Xu, X., Plaks, J. E., & Peterson, J. B. (2016). From dispositions to goals to ideology: Toward a synthesis of personality and social psychological approaches to political orientation. *Social and Personality Psychology Compass, 10*(5), 267–280. https://doi.org/10.1111/spc3.12248

Xu, X., Karinen, A. K., Chapman, H. A., Peterson, J. B., & Plaks, J. E. (2020). An orderly personality partially explains the link between trait disgust and political conservatism. *Cognition and Emotion, 34*(2), 302–315. https://doi.org/10.1080/02699931.2019.1627292

# 11

# What about Economic Attitudes, Extraversion, Agreeableness, and Neuroticism?

**Abstract** As the majority of the research has focused on the association between the Big Five and political orientations in terms of social attitudes, or a combination of social and economic attitudes, this chapter highlights the research that examines the association between personality and economic attitudes, as somewhat different findings are sometimes uncovered.

**Keywords** Personality • Trait theory • Big Five • Extraversion • Agreeableness • Compassion • Politeness • Neuroticism • Political orientations • Left-wing • Right-wing

As seen from Chap. 5, political attitudes include opinions on social issues, as well as economic issues. The research in the previous two chapters have largely focused on associations between personality and social attitudes or a combination of social and economic attitudes. However, when looking only at economic attitudes, somewhat different findings are sometimes uncovered. According to some research, left-wing economic attitudes are correlated positively with Openness, Agreeableness, and Neuroticism, but negatively with Conscientiousness (Carney et al., 2008; Gerber et al., 2010, 2011; Thorisdottir et al., 2007; Van Hiel & Mervielde, 2004). Given that those high in Conscientiousness are dutiful, industrious, and self-disciplined, it may be the case that they think those who work hard will get ahead (Bakker, 2014). Those who support right-wing economic policies are more tolerant of inequality (Jost, 2006; Jost et al., 2003, 2008, 2009). This may be because, if they are more conscientious, they accept inequality as a result of differences in achievement (Bakker, 2014). Similarly, left-wing economic policies will likely result in a change to the status quo. It is not surprising that support for this is positively associated with Openness, given that open individuals are more willing to try and consider new ideas (McCrae & Sutin, 2009).

Neuroticism encompasses feelings of anxiety, anger, depression, insecurity, and shyness (Costa & McCrae, 1992). While some research has found a positive association between Neuroticism and left-wing economic attitudes (Gerber et al., 2010 2011; Verhulst et al., 2012), other studies have failed to do so (Carney et al., 2008, Leeson & Heaven, 1999; Van Hiel & Mervielde, 2004). The potential relationship has been explained by suggesting that more neurotic individuals may support left-wing economic policies to create safety nets for themselves and reduce anxiety (Gerber et al., 2010, p. 116; Verhulst et al., 2012). However, research has not been able to confirm a connection between Anxiety (a facet of Neuroticism) and left-wing attitudes (Butler, 2000; Carney et al., 2008; Gerber et al., 2011). The relationship between Neuroticism and political orientations, therefore, is both inconsistent and unclear.

The connection between Extraversion and politics is even more hazy. Some studies have found North American liberals to be more extraverted than conservatives, especially in terms of being assertive and high in pleasure-seeking (Block & Block, 2006; Costantini & Craik, 1980; Fraley et al., 2012; Looft, 1971; McClosky, 1958). However, other research has documented a positive association between Extraversion and right-wing economic attitudes (Boozer & Forte, 2007; Gerber et al., 2010). Extraversion is, though, a clear mediator when it comes to taking part in rallies and protests (Mondak & Halperin, 2008; Ribeiro & Borba, 2016).

Agreeable individuals are known for being cooperative, altruistic, and sympathetic (Goldberg, 1981). Therefore, it has been theorized that Agreeableness is positively linked with left-wing economic attitudes due to agreeable individuals having greater sympathy for more disadvantaged people (Caprara et al., 2012). Indeed, there is a consistent relationship between Agreeableness and left-wing economic attitudes (Gerber et al., 2010, 2011; Riemann et al., 1993; Van Hiel & Mervielde, 2004).

The relationship between personality traits and economic attitudes may be influenced by income, meaning that individuals with lower incomes tend to be more supportive of left-wing economic policies, regardless of their personality traits (Bakker, 2014).[1] According to Bakker (2014, p. 103), "high income earners with low conscientiousness or high agreeableness have more liberal economic attitudes compared to high income earners with low agreeableness or high conscientiousness." Interestingly, this conclusion was based on results of two samples of participants, one in Denmark and one in the US, two counties with remarkably different economic policies.

More interestingly, Agreeableness is associated with left-wing political views more broadly than just economic attitudes. Earlier studies failed to find a relationship between Agreeableness and views on social issues, despite the fact that empathy is a strong component of Agreeableness and that social progressiveness is characterized as including low tolerance for inequality (Jost, 2006; Jost et al., 2003). However, more recent research using two aspects of Agreeableness (Compassion and Politeness), in accordance with the personality model by DeYoung (2006), have generated more robust findings. Specifically, Compassion is positively linked with progressiveness, while Politeness is linked with conservatism (Hirsh et al., 2010). Additionally, Agreeableness, as well as separate measures of compassion and empathy, predicted early vaccine acceptance during the COVID-19 pandemic (Murphy et al., 2021). Thus, previous research failed to recognize the importance of Agreeableness in relation to political orientations, as the two aspects of the dimension have divergent associations.

---

[1] The reader may want to note that Conscientiousness and Extraversion are positively associated with income, whereas Agreeableness and Neuroticism predict lower income (Judge et al., 1999; Ng et al., 2005; Sutin et al., 2009).

This fits nicely with the findings discussed in Chap. 6, including that those who endorse left-wing policies rely most heavily on the moral foundations of Care and Fairness when making moral decisions, since compassionate individuals report higher empathy and prosocial behavior. Therefore, it makes sense they would be motivated to take part in left-wing movements, specifically those related to equality. Polite individuals, on the other hand, are more likely to be compliant, cooperative, and respectful. This would explain why they are more likely to be loyal to tradition and show respect to authority.

The research outlined in this chapter highlights the most obvious limitations of research studying associations between personality and political orientations. First, research often relies upon one-dimensional models of political orientation, even though a multi-dimensional model consisting of a social attitude dimension and an economic attitude dimension is a more meaningful representation of political ideologies (Achterberg & Houtman, 2009; Conover & Feldman, 1981; Evans et al., 1996; Feldman & Johnston, 2014; Treier & Hillygus, 2009; Van Der Brug & Van Spanje, 2009). Though sometimes there is a correlation between social attitudes and economic attitudes, it is not always the case. Openness reliably predicts both social and economic left-wing attitudes. On the other hand, Agreeableness is positively associated with left-wing economic attitudes, but only Compassion is positively associated with left-wing social attitudes, not Agreeableness in general. Social conservatism is reliably associated with low Openness and high Conscientiousness, but economic conservatism is only sometimes linked to high Conscientiousness. Similarly, Neuroticism is sometimes associated with left-wing economic attitudes, but these findings are inconsistent, and the relationship between Extraversion and political orientation is unclear at this time, perhaps largely due to researchers using only one-dimensional models of political orientation in their studies.

The second most significant limitation is that the Big Five are sometimes treated by researchers as homogeneous dimensions. Using Costa and McCrae's model of personality, each Big Five personality trait consists of six lower order facets. Researchers often explain the association between the Big Five personality traits and political attitudes by focusing on only one of the facets, ignoring the others. More recently, researchers have discovered they can more accurately and reliably capture the association between personality and political attitudes by using DeYoung's model, breaking each of the five dimensions into two aspects. For instance, researchers often predict a significant association between Agreeableness and social attitudes, yet fail to find one (Alper & Yilmaz, 2019). The reason is that the two aspects of Agreeableness diverge in their associations with political ideology (i.e., Compassion is associated with progressiveness, and Politeness is associated with conservatism). Similarly, Orderliness predicts social conservatism, but not Industriousness, and Openness-to-experience predicts social progressiveness, but Intellect does not.

# Summary

The association between political orientations and Openness and Conscientious are more robust than other associations between politics and the remaining dimensions of the Big Five. There is some suggestion that the Big Five Aspects Scale taps into observations not observed with other methods. For instance, Agreeableness in general is not associated with either endorsement of left-wing or right-wing social policies, but Compassion correlates with left-wing endorsements and Politeness correlates with right-wing endorsements. Therefore, future research in this field is encouraged to continue this line of discovery by looking for associations between voting behavior and the ten aspects of the Big Five.

# References

Achterberg, P., & Houtman, D. (2009). Ideologically illogical? Why do the lower-educated Dutch display so little value coherence? *Social Forces, 87*(3), 1649–1670. https://doi.org/10.1353/sof.0.0164

Alper, S., & Yilmaz, O. (2019). How is the big five related to moral and political convictions: The moderating role of the WEIRDness of the culture. *Personality and Individual Differences, 145*, 32–38. https://doi.org/10.1016/j.paid.2019.03.018

Bakker, B. N. (2014). *Personality and politics*. [Doctoral dissertation]. University of Southern Denmark. http://www.sdu.dk/-/media/files/om_sdu/institutter/statskundskab/sidipob/phd+thesis+personality+and+politics.pdf

Block, J., & Block, J. H. (2006). Nursery school personality and political orientation two decades later. *Journal of Research in Personality, 40*(5), 734–749. https://doi.org/10.1016/j.jrp.2005.09.005

Boozer, R. W., & Forte, M. (2007). The relationship of psychological type to political self-perceptions, political opinions, and political party membership. *Journal of Psychological Type, 67*(3), 17–29.

Butler, J. C. (2000). Personality and emotional correlates of right-wing authoritarianism. *Social Behavior and Personality: An International Journal, 28*(1), 1–14. https://doi.org/10.2224/sbp.2000.28.1.1

Caprara, G. V., Alessandri, G., & Eisenberg, N. (2012). Prosociality: The contribution of traits, values, and self-efficacy beliefs. *Journal of Personality and Social Psychology, 102*(6), 1289–1303. https://doi.org/10.1037/a0025626

Carney, D. R., Jost, J. T., Gosling, S. D., & Potter, J. (2008). The secret lives of liberals and conservatives: Personality profiles, interaction styles, and the things they leave behind. *Political Psychology, 29*(6), 807–840. https://doi.org/10.1111/j.1467-9221.2008.00668.x

Conover, P. J., & Feldman, S. (1981). The origins and meaning of liberal/conservative self-identifications. *American Journal of Political Science, 25*(4), 617–645. https://doi.org/10.2307/2110756

Costa, P. T., & McCrae, R. R. (1992). *NEO PI-R professional manual*. Psychological Assessment Resources.

Costantini, E., & Craik, K. H. (1980). Personality and politicians: California party leaders, 1960–1976. *Journal of Personality and Social Psychology, 38*(4), 641–661. https://doi.org/10.1037/0022-3514.38.4.641

DeYoung, C. G. (2006). Higher-order factors of the big five in a multi-informant sample. *Journal of Personality and Social Psychology, 91*(6), 1138–1151. https://doi.org/10.1037/0022-3514.91.6.1138

Evans, G., Heath, A., & Lalljee, M. (1996). Measuring left-right and libertarian-authoritarian values in the British electorate. *British Journal of Sociology, 47*(1), 93–112. https://doi.org/10.2307/591118

Feldman, S., & Johnston, C. (2014). Understanding the determinants of political ideology: Implications of structural complexity. *Political Psychology, 35*(3), 337–358. https://doi.org/10.1111/pops.12055

Fraley, R. C., Griffin, B. N., Belsky, J., & Roisman, G. I. (2012). Developmental antecedents of political ideology: A longitudinal investigation from birth to age 18 years. *Psychological Science, 23*(11), 1425–1431. https://psycnet.apa.org/doi/10.1177/0956797612440102

Gerber, A. S., Huber, G. A., Doherty, D., & Dowling, C. M. (2011). The big five personality traits in the political arena. *Annual Review of Political Science, 14*, 265–287.

Gerber, A. S., Huber, G. A., Doherty, D., Dowling, C. M., & Ha, S. E. (2010). Personality and political attitudes: Relationships across issue domains and political contexts. *American Political Science Review, 104*, 111.

Goldberg, L. K. (1981). Language and individual differences: The search for universals in personality lexicons. In L. Wheeler (Ed.), *Review of personality and social psychology* (Vol. 2, pp. 141–165). Sage.

Hirsh, J. B., DeYoung, C. G., Xu, X., & Peterson, J. B. (2010). Compassionate liberals and polite conservatives: Associations of agreeableness with political ideology and moral values. *Personality and Social Psychology Bulletin, 36*(5), 655–664. https://doi.org/10.1177/0146167210366854

Jost, J. T. (2006). The end of the end of ideology. *American Psychologist, 61*(7), 651–670. https://doi.org/10.1037/0003-066X.61.7.651

Jost, J. T., Glaser, J., Kruglanski, A. W., & Sulloway, F. J. (2003). Political conservatism as motivated social cognition. *Psychological Bulletin, 129*(3), 339–375. https://doi.org/10.1037/0033-2909.129.3.339

Jost, J. T., Nosek, B. A., & Gosling, S. D. (2008). Ideology: Its resurgence in social, personality, and political psychology. *Perspectives on Psychological Science, 3*(2), 126–136. https://doi.org/10.1111/j.1745-6916.2008.00070.x

Jost, J. T., West, T. V., & Gosling, S. D. (2009). Personality and ideology as determinants of candidate preferences and "Obama conversion" in the 2008 US presidential election. *Du Bois Review: Social Science Research on Race, 6*(1), 103–124. https://doi.org/10.1017/S1742058X09090109

Judge, T. A., Higgins, C. A., Thoresen, C. J., & Barrick, M. R. (1999). The big five personality traits, general mental ability, and career success across the life span. *Personnel Psychology, 52*(3), 621–652. https://doi.org/10.1111/j.1744-6570.1999.tb00174.x

Leeson, P., & Heaven, P. C. (1999). Social attitudes and personality. *Australian Journal of Psychology, 51*(1), 19–24. https://doi.org/10.1080/000495 39908255330

Looft, W. R. (1971). Conservatives, liberals, radicals, and sensation-seekers. *Perceptual and Motor Skills, 32*(1), 98. https://doi.org/10.2466/pms.1971.32.1.98

McClosky, H. (1958). Conservatism and personality. *American Political Science Review, 52*(1), 27–45. https://doi.org/10.2307/1953011

McCrae, R. R., & Sutin, A. R. (2009). Openness to experience. In M. R. Leary & R. H. Hoyle (Eds.), *Handbook of individual differences in social behavior* (pp. 257–273). The Guilford Press.

Mondak, J. J., & Halperin, K. D. (2008). A framework for the study of personality and political behaviour. *British Journal of Political Science, 23*, 443–455. https://doi.org/10.1038/s41593-020-0600-3

Murphy, J., Vallières, F., Bentall, R. P., Shevlin, M., McBride, O., Hartman, T. K., et al. (2021). Psychological characteristics associated with COVID-19 vaccine hesitancy and resistance in Ireland and the United Kingdom. *Nature Communications, 12*(1), 29. https://doi.org/10.1038/s41467-020-20226-9

Ng, T. W. H., Eby, L. T., Sorensen, K. L., & Feldman, D. C. (2005). Predictors of objective and subjective career success. A meta-analysis. *Personnel Psychology, 58*(2), 367–408. https://doi.org/10.1111/j.1744-6570.2005.00515.x

Ribeiro, A. E., & Borba, J. (2016). Personality, political attitudes and participation in protests: The direct and mediated effects of psychological factors on political activism. *Brazilian Political Science Review, 10*(3), 1–33. https://doi.org/10.1590/1981-38212016000300003

Riemann, R., Grubich, C., Hempel, S., Mergl, S., & Richter, M. (1993). Personality and attitudes towards current political topics. *Personality and Individual Differences, 15*(3), 313–321. https://doi.org/10.1016/0191-8869(93)90222-O

Sutin, A. R., Costa, P. T., Jr., Miech, R., & Eaton, W. W. (2009). Personality and career success: Concurrent and longitudinal relations. *European Journal of Personality, 23*(2), 71–84. https://doi.org/10.1002/per.704

Thorisdottir, H., Jost, J. T., Liviatan, I., & Shrout, P. E. (2007). Psychological needs and values underlying left-right political orientation: Cross-national evidence from eastern and Western Europe. *Public Opinion Quarterly, 71*(2), 175–203. https://doi.org/10.1093/poq/nfm008

Treier, S., & Hillygus, D. S. (2009). The nature of political ideology in the contemporary electorate. *Public Opinion Quarterly, 73*(4), 679–703. https://doi.org/10.1093/poq/nfp067

Van der Brug, W., & Van Spanje, J. (2009). Immigration, Europe and the 'new' cultural dimension. *European Journal of Political Research, 48*(3), 309–334. https://doi.org/10.1111/j.1475-6765.2009.00841.x

Van Hiel, A., & Mervielde, I. (2004). Openness to experience and boundaries in the mind: Relationships with cultural and economic conservative beliefs. *Journal of Personality, 72*(4), 659–686. https://doi.org/10.1111/j.0022-3506.2004.00276.x

Verhulst, B., Eaves, L. J., & Hatemi, P. K. (2012). Correlation not causation: The relationship between personality traits and political ideologies. *American Journal of Political Science, 56*(1), 34–51. https://doi.org/10.1111/j.1540-5907.2011.00568.x

# 12

# Authoritarianism

**Abstract** In this chapter, a brief history is presented of how psychologists have attempted to understand the concept of authoritarianism. It also explores the relationship between Right-Wing Authoritarianism and Social Dominance Orientation and their association with political attitudes and personality traits.

**Keywords** Personality • Trait theory • Authoritarianism • Right-Wing Authoritarianism (RWA) • Social Dominance Orientation (SDO) • Prejudice

An authoritarian personality refers to a combined longing for power over others and a yearning for submission to an overwhelming, outside authority (Tudoroiu, 2017). The concept was developed by Erich Fromm, a psychoanalyst, who blended the ideas of Sigmund Freud and Karl Marx to create a compromise between Freud's emphasis on unconscious biological drives and Marx's view that people are simply products of their society. In Fromm's view, freedom is central to human nature, and people have the ability to overcome the personality impactors proposed by Freud and Marx. The concept of authoritarianism was intended to explain the rise of fascism in the 1930s, in which individuals displayed extreme obedience and submission to the authority of totalitarian governments, realized through the oppression of other individuals. The concept of an authoritarian personality was further developed by a book, co-authored in 1950 by Adorno, Frenkel-Brunswik, Levinson, and Sanford, using psychoanalytic theories as a framework, to concentrate on explanations of prejudice, including the rise of antisemitism in Nazi Germany.

Psychoanalytic theories emphasize the significance of unconscious motives and drives in explaining human behavior. Sigmund Freud, who is regarded as the founder of psychoanalytic theory, used the metaphor of an iceberg to depict the human mind. He suggested that only a small part of the mind is observable, while the majority of it is submerged (or unconscious). According to Freud's theory, there are three components of personality. First, the id is the most primitive part of the psyche, characterized by animalistic drives and primal desires. Second, the ego develops to regulate the id's impulses, as individuals cannot always obtain what they desire. The ego determines what one can realistically obtain. Lastly, the superego serves as the guardian of societal values. Each of these components has its own objectives. For instance, if the person in front of you drops a bill of money, the id might act like a devil on your shoulder, urging you to take it and flee. The superego, on the other hand, may behave like an angel, reminding you that stealing is immoral. The ego will consider both arguments and reach a conclusion.

In psychoanalytic theory, individuals with an authoritarian personality are characterized by a strict superego that exerts control over a weak ego, which is unable to mediate the demands of the id. Neurotic anxiety is the result of one feeling as though they cannot control their id. The outcome of this, in an authoritarian personality, is that the person, listening to the demands of their superego, adheres to the imposed conventional norms, offering unquestioned obedience to the authority who imposes the social norms of society. This anxiety also causes a cynical view of humanity. Authoritarian individuals tend to focus on those who violate social norms and believe that a strong power is necessary to ensure compliance with conventions. Adorno et al. (1950) argue that authoritarian personality is developed during the first year of a person's life, as a result of growing up with authoritarian parents who are domineering and harshly threaten their children to conform to conventional behaviors.

The California F-scale, created by Adorno in 1947, is used to measure authoritarianism. High scores on the F-scale indicate individuals who exhibit conventional, rigid, hostile, and aggressive behavior towards those who deviate from social norms (Jost & Sidanius, 2004). While initial responses to Adorno's scale were enthusiastic, Adorno's work eventually came under heavy criticism for a number of reasons. First of all, the measurement scales worked for ring-wing authoritarianism, but not for left-wing authoritarianism. Furthermore, the scale was formed based upon non-representative samples and was criticized for being poorly constructed (Tudoroiu, 2017). Critics also argued that Adorno and colleagues could not demonstrate the origin of authoritarianism in early parent-child interactions as they claimed. Finally, an actual assessment of 16 Nazi criminals at Nuremberg trials found that they did not score highly on the majority of the F-scale's dimensions (Zillmer et al., 1995).

Interest in the subject was revitalized by Bob Altemeyer in 1988, a trait theorist, who constructed the Right-Wing Authoritarianism (RWA) scale. The scale identifies three main clusters of personality characteristics: (1) submission to legitimate authorities, (2) aggression towards minority groups whom authorities identify as targets, (3) and adherence to political beliefs endorsed by authorities (McCrae & Costa, 1997). Given that people who score high in Openness tend to be liberal and tolerant of diversity (Carney et al., 2008; Sibley et al., 2012; Xu et al., 2013), it is not surprising that RWA correlates negatively with Openness (McCrae & Costa, 1997). Indeed, these individuals are more open to different cultures and lifestyles, reporting lower scores in ethnocentrism, RWA, Social Dominance Orientation, and prejudice than people lower in Openness (Sibley & Duckitt, 2008). In contrast, RWA is one of the strongest predictors of prejudice (Chen and Palmer 2017; Sibley & Duckitt, 2008).

Studies indicate that individuals with high RWA scores are less likely to engage in critical thinking and are more inclined to blame a scapegoat for a country's problems once one is identified. They are also prone to disregarding inconsistencies (Tudoroiu, 2017). Altemeyer (1998, 2004) suggests that social learning theory better explains the development of RWA than psychoanalytic theory, asserting that negative attitudes and discriminatory behaviors are learned from adults. Children may adopt the same attitudes as their parents to be accepted by them, as they have a strong desire to be loved. The RWA has stronger psychometric properties than its F-scale predecessor and has clear political implications. For example, those scoring higher on RWA are more likely to support controls on personal freedom and hold hostility towards perceived out-groups, such as homosexuals and feminists (Altemeyer, 1996; Meloen, 1996).

Another explanation that examines the association between personality and attitudes towards group-related hierarchies is social dominance theory, developed in the 1990s. It is based on the theory that societies can minimize group conflict and ethnocentrism by decreasing intergroup inequality. The Social Dominance Orientation (SDO) scale was created in 1994 by Patto, Sidanius, Stallworth, and Malle to measure one's social dominance orientation. Those who score highly on this scale are those who believe some people are meant to dominate and want to be the ones who dominate. Therefore, they are more likely to favor unequal, hierarchical, dominance-orientated relationships among groups. Researchers have suggested that SDO develops as a result of cold, insensitive caregivers during childhood (Whitley & Kite, 2010). Although the SDO scale predicts similar outcomes to the RWA scale, it is worth noting that SDO does not predict higher religiosity, unlike RWA (Whitley, 1999).

Although RWA and SDO have similar predictions of socio-political and intergroup phenomena, they are weakly correlated with each other (Tudoroiu, 2017). To explain this, Altemeyer has suggested that they measure two different authoritarian personalities: a submissive type and a dominant type. Consequently, it has been argued that totalitarian leaders who possess a dominant type of authoritarian personality, such as Hitler, Mao, and Castro, exhibit high levels of SDO (Tudoroiu, 2017). These leaders aimed to instill fear in others, treated out-groups with hostility and inferiority, and promoted intense competition among their close associates. Although not all of them were right-wing, they were all totalitarian leaders who shared similar personality traits.

Altemeyer (1996) argues that the submission to authority that characterizes high RWA scorers, as well as aggression against nonconformist groups, helps to explain why some individuals are more susceptible to following orders of fascist regimes, such as that of Nazi Germany, as well as the rabid antisemitic ideologies of that regime. However, other studies have shown that it is not only high RWA scorers who respond strongly to orders from authority. Julian Rotter developed the theory that some people believe reinforcers depend on their own actions, while other people believe reinforcers are controlled by outside forces. He called this locus of control. Those who believe that the reinforcement they receive is under the control of their own behavior are characterized as internal locus of control personalities, whereas those who believe that the rewards they receive are due to outside forces are characterized as having an external locus of control. Research shows that internal personalities are more likely to resist authority than externals (Blass, 1991).

The series of experiments by Stanley Milgram are the most well-known for demonstrating the power of authority. He led participants to believe they were being asked to send increasingly strong electric shocks into another participant. Shockingly, people often complied even when asked to shoot more than 400 volts of electricity. This led researchers to theorize that everyone is capable of following orders, no matter how evil, if the conditions are right. Milgram found that the chances of a participant cooperating were increased by a number of factors. For example, there was a higher chance of a participant complying if they could not see or hear the person they were shocking. However, Milgram's experiments also revealed that 35% of participants refused to administer the most severe shocks, a fact that is often overlooked. Therefore, if Milgram's study samples are representative, approximately one-third of people are inclined to disobey authority. Indeed, personality plays a role, as Elms and Milgram (1966) found that people higher in authoritarianism were more likely to comply.

Clearly, personality is not the only factor that plays a role. The dynamics of a group matter. The more people in a group, the more individual responsibility is diffused, referred to as the bystander effect. Milgram also found that a participant was more likely to refuse if they witnessed another participant also refuse to take part. There are a number of parallels between Milgram's studies and the case of Nazi Germany. In Nazi Germany, depersonalization was an important part in facilitating genocide. The camps were organized in a way in which personal identification with the victims was unnecessary. Furthermore, the process was divided into so many smaller roles that those taking part were able to lessen their own personal responsibility. In Milgram's studies, participants sometimes asked the experimenter if they would take responsibility if something happened to the shockee. When the experimenter responded that they would, this seemed to give the green light to continue.

However, the reasons for why German soldiers followed orders during World War Two run deeper than group-related factors. Looking at the research findings outlined in Chap. 10, it is not hard to imagine how the association between behavior and underlying biology can be hijacked and used for political agendas. Following the Black Plague in Europe, for instance, Jews were preposterously blamed for the outbreak, accused of poisoning wells, and tens of thousands of Jewish people were massacred across Europe. Before Hitler's rise to power, Germany was a disordered nation, financially destroyed by the punitive Treaty of Versailles and devastated by diseases that had spread from the trenches, including the Spanish Flu (which killed more people than the entire war). Hitler rose to power partly as a result of celebrating German nationalism, demonstrating his in-group quality, and also by promising to purify Germany and to provide order. Furthermore, he provided a scapegoat in order to increase group esteem. Understanding the various effects of prejudice will hopefully help to fight against it, no matter where one falls on the political spectrum.

Importantly, authoritarianism, even RWA, and conservatism are not synonymous (Crowson et al., 2005). Though both stems from a predisposition towards social conformity, RWA is rooted in a view of the world being a dangerous place, thereby increasing cognitive rigidity on conservative attitudes (Crowson et al., 2005; Duckitt, 2001; Duckitt & Sibley, 2010; Osborne et al., 2017). Consistent with this argument is that increases in levels of threat cause an increase in authoritarianism, as well as support for authoritarian leaders and policies (Bonanno & Jost, 2006; Duckitt & Fisher, 2003; McCann, 1997; Sales, 1972; Stellmacher & Petzel, 2005). On the other hand, SDO stems from a view that the world is a competitive jungle, creating intergroup struggle for dominance and superiority (Crawford & Pilanski, 2014). Evidence suggests that RWA more strongly predicts conservative attitudes on social political issues, while SDO more strongly predicts conservative attitudes on economic political issues (Altemeyer, 1998; Duriez & Van Hiel, 2002; Van Hiel &

Mervielde, 2002; Van Hiel et al., 2004). For example, RWA more strongly predicts conservative views on same-sex relationships, whereas SDO more strongly predicts conservative opinions on affirmative action (Crawford et al., 2013). Both, therefore, have the potential to impact prejudice in different ways. RWA bolsters prejudice in the presence of an increased sense of threat, such as fake news about immigrants increasing crime rates, while SDO more strongly predicts higher prejudice under conditions of greater competition, such as in countries with higher unemployment rates (Duckitt & Sibley, 2010).

## Summary

RWA and SDO are distinct personality traits that can impact voting patterns by influencing the expression of prejudice and the support for political policies that promote intolerance. These traits differ in their focus, with RWA more closely linked to attitudes on social issues and SDO more closely linked to attitudes on economic issues.

## Exercises

You may complete the Right-Wing Authoritarianism Scale here: https://www.idrlabs.com/right-wing-authoritarianism/test.php.

## References

Adorno, T. W., Frenkel-Brunswik, E., Levinson, D. J., & Sanford, R. N. (1950). *The authoritarian personality*. Harper and Row.
Altemeyer, B. (1996). *The authoritarian specter*. Harvard University Press.
Altemeyer, B. (1998). The other "authoritarian personality". *Advances in Experimental Social Psychology, 30*, 47–92. https://doi.org/10.1016/S0065-2601(08)60382-2
Altemeyer, B. (2004). Highly dominating, highly authoritarian personalities. *The Journal of Social Psychology, 144*(4), 421–447. https://doi.org/10.3200/SOCP.144.4.421-448

Blass, T. (1991). Understanding behavior in the Milgram obedience experiment: The role of personality, situations, and their interactions. *Journal of Personality and Social Psychology, 60*(3), 398–413. https://doi.org/10.1037/0022-3514.60.3.398

Bonanno, G. A., & Jost, J. T. (2006). Conservative shift among high-exposure survivors of the September 11th terrorist attacks. *Basic and Applied Social Psychology, 28*(4), 311–323. https://doi.org/10.1207/s15324834basp2804_4

Carney, D. R., Jost, J. T., Gosling, S. D., & Potter, J. (2008). The secret lives of liberals and conservatives: Personality profiles, interaction styles, and the things they leave behind. *Political Psychology, 29*(6), 807–840. https://doi.org/10.1111/j.1467-9221.2008.00668.x

Chen, P., & Palmer, C. L. (2017). The prejudiced personality? Using the big five to predict susceptibility to stereotyping behavior. *American Politics Research, 46*, 276–307.

Crawford, J. T., Jussim, L., Cain, T. R., & Cohen, F. (2013). Right-wing authoritarianism and social dominance orientation differentially predict biased evaluations of media reports. *Journal of Applied Social Psychology, 43*(1), 163–174. https://doi.org/10.1111/j.1559-1816.2012.00990.x

Crawford, J. T., & Pilanski, J. M. (2014). The differential effects of right-wing authoritarianism and social dominance orientation on political intolerance. *Political Psychology, 35*(4), 557–576.

Crowson, H. M., Thoma, S. J., & Hestevold, N. (2005). Is political conservatism synonymous with authoritarianism? *The Journal of Social Psychology, 145*(5), 571–592. https://doi.org/10.3200/SOCP.145.5.571-592

Duckitt, J. (2001). A dual-process cognitive-motivational theory of ideology and prejudice. In M. P. Zanna (Ed.), *Advances in experimental social psychology* (Vol. 33, pp. 41–113). Academic Press.

Duckitt, J., & Fisher, K. (2003). Social threat, worldview, and ideological attitudes. *Political Psychology, 24*, 199–222.

Duckitt, J., & Sibley, C. G. (2010). Right-wing authoritarianism and social dominance orientation differentially moderate intergroup effects on prejudice. *European Journal of Personality, 24*(7), 583–601. https://doi.org/10.1002/per.772

Duriez, B., & Van Hiel, A. (2002). The march of modern fascism. A comparison of social dominance orientation and authoritarianism. *Personality and Individual Differences, 32*(7), 1199–1213. https://doi.org/10.1016/S0191-8869(01)00086-1

Elms, A. C., & Milgram, S. (1966). Personality characteristics associated with obedience and defiance toward authoritative command. *Journal of Experimental Research in Personality, 1,* 282–289.

Jost, J. T., & Sidanius, J. (2004). *Political psychology: An introduction.* Psychology Press.

McCann, S. J. H. (1997). Threatening times, "strong" presidential popular vote winners, and the victory margin, 1824–1964. *Journal of Personality and Social Psychology, 73*(1), 160–170. https://doi.org/10.1037/0022-3514.73.1.160

McCrae, R. R., & Costa, P. T., Jr. (1997). Conceptions and correlates of openness to experience. In R. Hogan, J. A. Johnson, & S. R. Briggs (Eds.), *Handbook of personality psychology* (pp. 825–847). Academic.

Meloen, J. (1996). Authoritarianism, democracy, and education. In R. F. Farnen, H. Dekker, R. Meyenberg, & D. B. German (Eds.), *Democracy, socialization and conflicting loyalties in east and west* (pp. 20–38). Palgrave Macmillan. https://doi.org/10.1007/978-1-349-14059-6_2

Osborne, D., Milojev, P., & Sibley, C. G. (2017). Authoritarianism and national identity: Examining the longitudinal effects of SDO and RWA on nationalism and patriotism. *Personality and Social Psychology, 43*(8), 1086–1099. https://doi.org/10.1177/0146167217704196

Pratto, F., Sidanius, J., Stallworth, L. M., & Malle, B. F. (1994). Social dominance orientation: A personality variable predicting social and political attitudes. *Journal of Personality and Social Psychology, 67*(4), 741–763. https://doi.org/10.1037/0022-3514.67.4.741

Sales, S. M. (1972). Economic threat as a determinant of conversion rates in authoritarian and nonauthoritarian churches. *Journal of Personality and Social Psychology, 23*(3), 420–428. https://doi.org/10.1037/h0033157

Sibley, C. G., & Duckitt, J. (2008). Personality and prejudice: A meta-analysis and theoretical review. *Personality and Social Psychology Review, 12*(3), 248–279. https://doi.org/10.1177/1088868308319226

Sibley, C. G., Osborne, D., & Duckitt, J. (2012). Personality and political orientation: Meta-analysis and test of a threat-constraint model. *Journal of Research in Personality, 46*(6), 664–677. https://doi.org/10.1016/j.jrp.2012.08.002

Stellmacher, J., & Petzel, T. (2005). Authoritarianism as a group phenomenon. *Political Psychology, 26,* 245–274. https://doi.org/10.1111/j.1467-9221.2005.00417.x

Tudoroiu, T. (2017). *The revolutionary totalitarian personality: Hitler, Mao, Castro, and Chávez.* Springer.

Van Hiel, A., & Mervielde, I. (2002). Explaining conservative beliefs and political preferences: A comparison of social dominance orientation and authoritarianism. *Journal of Applied Social Psychology, 32*, 965–976. https://doi.
org/10.1111/j.1559-1816.2002.tb00250.x

Van Hiel, A., Pandelaere, M., & Duriez, B. (2004). The impact of need for closure on conservative beliefs and racism: Differential mediation by authoritarian submission and authoritarian dominance. *Personality and Social Psychology
Bulletin, 30*(7), 824–837. https://doi.org/10.1177/0146167204264333

Whitley, B. E., Jr. (1999). Right-wing authoritarianism, social dominance orientation, and prejudice. *Journal of Personality and Social Psychology, 77*(1),
126–134. https://doi.org/10.1037/0022-3514.77.1.126

Whitley, B. E., Jr., & Kite, M. E. (2010). *The psychology of prejudice and discrimi-
nation* (2nd ed.). Wadsworth.

Xu, X., Mar, R. A., & Peterson, J. B. (2013). Does cultural exposure partially
explain the association between personality and political orientation?
*Personality and Social Psychology Bulletin, 39*(11), 1497–1517. https://doi.
org/10.1177/0146167213499235

Zillmer, E. A., Harrower, M., Ritzler, B., & Archer, R. P. (1995). *The quest for
the Nazi personality: A psychological investigation of Nazi war criminals*. Erlbaum.

# 13

# Political Correctness: Authoritarianism and White Identitarianism

**Abstract** This chapter outlines recent research findings by Moss and O'Connor on two new forms of authoritarianism, intended to capture the ideologies of the "Regressive Left" and "Alt Right."

**Keywords** Authoritarianism • Political Correctness-Authoritarianism • White Identitarianism • Regressive-left • Alt-right

Two recent forms of authoritarianism that have been proposed are Political Correctness-Authoritarianism, capturing the ideology of the "Regressive Left," and White Identitarianism, describing attitudes held by the "Alt-Right," to describe more contemporary political attitudes at the extreme ends of the political spectrum. Just as the horseshoe theory argues, Moss and O'Connor (2020a) claim, based upon their research in the United States, that these two extremes have more in common with one another than they do with those with more moderate political views. For instance, both correlate with measures of black-white thinking, entitlement, narcissism, and psychopathy (Moss & O'Connor,

© The Author(s), under exclusive license to Springer Nature Switzerland AG 2023
B. F. Cotterill, *Personality Psychology, Ideology, and Voting Behavior: Beyond the Ballot*,
https://doi.org/10.1007/978-3-031-39642-7_13

2020a; Moss & O'Connor, 2020). Moss and O'Connor (2020a, 2020b), therefore, argue that authoritarianism can be seen on both sides of the left-right dimension.

Political correctness refers to a desire to suppress offensive language and threats to egalitarianism (Andary-Brophy, 2015; Moss & O'Connor, 2020a). It is predicted by high Agreeableness, specifically Compassion, and Openness, and is associated with the left of the political spectrum (Andary-Brophy, 2015; Moss & O'Connor, 2020a). Lukianoff and Haidt (2018) theorized that social media usage and overprotective parenting were significant contributors to endorsing political correctness. Indeed, Moss and O'Connor (2020a) found political correctness was predicted by greater social media usage. They found no evidence that overprotective parenting contributed to having politically correct views, but did find it significantly predicted Political Correctness-Authoritarianism.

Political Correctness-Authoritarianism (PCA) refers to a belief that it is appropriate to use aggression and force to achieve the goals of political correctness (Andary-Brophy, 2015). Psychopathy, characterized by anti-social behavior and a lack of care for others, is a positive predictor of PCA, but a negative predictor of political correctness more generally (Moss & O'Connor, 2020). Furthermore, PCA correlates with entitlement and narcissism, and is predicted by rigid black-and-white moral thinking and a lack of resilience (Moss & O'Connor, 2020a; Moss & O'Connor, 2020). In regard to the Big Five, PCA is predicted by Agreeableness, specifically high Compassion, and low Politeness (Moss & O'Connor, 2020a). Congruent with findings by Moss and O'Connor (2020), Conway et al. (2018) also argued in favor of the existence of a left-wing authoritarianism trait, arguing that that there were similarities between those who scored highly in this trait and those who scored highly in RWA in regard to dogmatism and prejudice.

White Identitarianism (WI) refers to a strong belief in white solidarity and in white victimization (Moss & O'Connor, 2020). It is a viewpoint that has attracted a great deal of coverage in the media in recent years due to violent protests, such as the Charlottesville rally in August 2017. According to a 2018 survey, 60% of Americans saw white supremacists as a growing threat, and 80% saw political correctness as an issue, indicating that both WI and PCA are current matters of concern (Hawkins et al.,

2018). Similar to PCA, WI is also predicted by black-and-white thinking, entitlement, narcissism, and psychopathy (Moss & O'Connor, 2020a; Moss & O'Connor, 2020). It is also predicted by machiavellianism, referring to a willingness to be cunning and manipulative in order to gain power over others (Moss & O'Connor, 2020). In regard to the Big Five, it is negatively predicted by Openness and Agreeableness, specifically Politeness, and is positively predicted by Orderliness (Moss & O'Connor, 2020a). This is consistent with previous findings discussed in this text that those on the extreme right of the political spectrum are more likely to score higher in Orderliness and lower in Openness. Therefore, Moss and O'Connor (2020a) argue that WI is a valid term to represent the current far right in the United States.

## Summary

PCA and WI are concepts only recently studied, referring to current extreme political attitudes on the political left and right respectively. Most of the research has been conducted by a small handful of researchers using North American participants. As such, there is a need for further research to replicate and expand upon existing findings and to deepen our understanding of these phenomena.

## Exercises

You may here complete the Dark Triad Test, used to measure psychopathy, machiavellianism, and narcissism: https://www.idrlabs.com/dark-triad/test.php

## References

Andary-Brophy, C. A. (2015). *Political correctness: Social-fiscal liberalism and left-wing authoritarianism.* [Master's thesis]. University of Toronto. https://tspace.library.utoronto.ca/bitstream/1807/75755/3/Brophy_Christine_201511_MA_thesis.pdf

Conway, L. G., III, Houck, S. C., Gornick, L. J., & Repke, M. A. (2018). Finding the loch ness monster: Left-wing authoritarianism in the United States. *Political Psychology, 39*(5), 1049–1067. https://doi.org/10.1111/pops.12470

Hawkins, S., Yudkin, D., Juan-Torres, M., & Dixon, T. (2018). Hidden tribes: A study of America's polarized landscape. *More in Common.* https://static1. squarespace.com/static/5a70a7c3010027736a22740f/t/5b bcea6b7817f7bf7342b718/1539107467397/hidden_tribes_report-2.pdf

Moss, J. T., & O'Connor, P. J. (2020a). Political correctness and the alt-right: The development of extreme political attitudes. *PLoS One, 15*(10), e0239259. https://doi.org/10.1371/journal.pone.0239259

Moss, J., & O'Connor, P. J. (2020b). The dark triad traits predict authoritarian political correctness and alt-right attitudes. *Heliyon, 6*(7), e04453. https://doi.org/10.1016/j.heliyon.2020.e04453

# 14

# Social Psychological Explanations of Political Atrocities

**Abstract** While this text mainly focuses on dispositional explanations of political behavior, this chapter reminds the reader that situational factors also play a crucial role. This is particularly evident when trying to comprehend political atrocities such as the Holocaust. Christopher Browning's 1992 book, *Ordinary Men*, emphasizes various situational factors that influenced Holocaust perpetrators. This text argues that in extreme situations, personality appears to have less of an impact on behavior than in ordinary circumstances. In unordinary instances, people are often more likely to follow the norms of the group, as illustrated by studies on conformity and obedience to authority.

**Keywords** Social psychology • Group processes • Conformity • Peer pressure • Obedience to authority • Cognitive dissonance • the holocaust

To be clear, this text, so far, has focused largely on dispositional explanations of political behavior, but it is undeniable that situational factors are also important. In fact, it is often difficult to separate the two. This is perhaps no clearer than when trying to explain political atrocities, such as the Holocaust. In what is likely the most horrific event in human history, almost an entire country's population became complicit in the murder of six million Jews and five million prisoners of war via the liquidation of Jewish ghettos and the transportation to concentration camps. Early explanations of the Holocaust focused on personality-related factors, such as the Fascist-scale described in Chap. 12, but these were largely discredited. Daniel Goldhagen (author of *Hitler's Willing Executioners*, 1996) argues that Germans willingly took part in acts of genocide due to strong feelings of antisemitism that were unique to Germans at that time. Christopher Browning (author of *Ordinary Men*, 1992), however, emphasizes a variety of situational factors that influenced perpetrators during the Holocaust, and disputes the notion that there was one specific cause shared by the individuals. After all, the perpetrators of the Holocaust willingly murdered millions of non-Jews, so antisemitism cannot be the only explanation.

Instead, in the case of Reserve Police Battalion 101, Browning found that these 500 men were too old to have been significantly indoctrinated, though too young to have fought in World War One, meaning they were unlikely to be desensitized to violence, and were not particularly receptive to antisemitic propaganda. Therefore, this group of ordinary Germans were not likely candidates for perpetrators of mass murder. Indeed, many were hesitant to carry out their duties at the start of their conscription. By the end of the war, however, these 500 men had deported 45,000 Jews to the Treblinka concentration camp and personally executed 38,000 Jews via mass shootings and firing squads. The members of this battalion were able to recall the early killings with great clarity when giving testimony after the war. It seems, though, that the men quickly became desensitized to violence and that committing mass murder became almost banal, as their memory for specific details decreased and decreased as the executions went on.

The most important discovery concerning the testimonies of Reserve Police Battalion 101 was the finding that they were given a choice over whether or not to execute Jews. Many Nazis at the Nuremberg trials claimed they carried out their duties because they would have been executed otherwise, despite no evidence ever being presented to support these claims. On the contrary, letters from SS Leader Heinrich Himmler indicate he understood some men were unsuited for the task of mass murder and should have been reassigned. In the case of Reserve Police Battalion 101, there was no question that they were given the choice to step aside during mass killings. During the first executions, only 11 out of 500 men opted to sit out. The other members of the battalion saw that they went unpunished and that sitting out was a viable option. This raises questions, therefore, concerning the situational and social factors that contribute towards ordinary individuals behaving monstrously. In explanation, Browning discusses four main pieces of evidence: (1) Asch's conformity and peer pressure experiments, (2) Milgram's obedience to authority experiments, (3) Zimbardo's Stanford Prison Experiment, and (4) evidence of cognitive dissonance.

Browning argues that conformity and peer pressure played a vital role in turning otherwise ordinary German men into mass killers. He argues that few Germans approached their duty with an eagerness to kill unarmed civilians. Instead, Browning suggests that Germans were aware that their fellow battalion members would complete the tasks if they didn't, leading to a fear of being viewed as selfish or cowardly for not participating. Browning cites Solomon Asch's experiments as evidence of the human tendency to conform. In these studies, Asch presented participants in groups with a series of lines. Unknown to the participants, the other members of the group were confederates who were in on the experiment. The groups were asked questions regarding the length of the lines, and the confederates provided answers that were obviously incorrect. The participants were faced with the choice of disagreeing with the group by giving the correct response or conforming to the group's obviously false response. In one study, Asch found that 66% of participants conformed at least once and that nearly 40% of participants conformed in response to every question.

In contrast to Browning, Goldhagen (1996) offers a different perspective on conformity. He posits that the majority of the German men must have been willing executioners, as they would not have participated in mass murder if the group's prevailing view was against genocide. While there is a logic to Goldhagen's argument, it is likely too simplistic and ignores the complexity of the situation, including the dynamics of the group; after all, orders were coming from officers in favor of genocide, and sadists were strategically placed within the Nazi party into positions where they could do the most damage and have the most influence over others as possible.

As explained in the previous chapter, Milgram's obedience to authority experiments were a series of well-known studies demonstrating that ordinary people would inflict harm on strangers via administering a series of electric shocks when told to do so. Though they were able to stop at any time, 65% of participants in one study administered electric shocks at the highest possible voltage. Browning compared the massacre of Jews during the Holocaust as "a kind of radical Milgram experiment that took place in a Polish forest with real killers and victims rather than in a social psychology laboratory" (1992, pp. 173–174). As noted by Goldhagen, however, one issue with this comparison is that many subjects in Milgram's experiments followed orders hesitantly, while there is evidence that Germans often volunteered to massacre Jews during the Second World War. Furthermore, many eventually came to take pride and pleasure in tormenting and humiliating their victims before killing them.

It is important to note that German child-rearing practices during that time may have contributed to the situation. Although an authoritarian parenting style was prevalent in most Western countries at the turn of the twentieth century, parents in Germany were, on average, more physically abusive than in other nations, and the rates of infanticide in Germany were significantly higher than in France or the United Kingdom (DeMause, 2002). In fact, child suicide rates in Germany were three to five times higher than in other European nations, and historians suggest that the most common reason for these suicides was to avoid severe and persistent physical punishment from parents (DeMause, 2002). In pre-war Germany, newborns were separated from their mothers for the first 24 hours after birth, and Nazi physicians advised parents not to rush to their children when they cried or had difficulties (Haarer, 1937, as cited in Rowold, 2013). The intention was to prevent children from developing a bond with a nurturing caregiver and to encourage resilience. Indeed, as Chamberlain (2004, p. 368) explains, "German children were whipped, locked into dark rooms, and bound to tables. They were forced to kneel before a wall or stand in a corner for hours. They were endlessly frightened by tales of wild figures, black men who would fetch the child if it didn't behave. They were supposed to be 'hardened' by the constant application of ice-cold water." As a result, not only did German children grow up frightened of authority, but the coldness they experienced in childhood also increased the risk of them having antisocial tendencies in adulthood (Chamberlain, 2004).

According to Goldhagen (1996), the behavior of Holocaust perpetrators was shaped mainly by dispositional factors, such as their antisemitic attitudes and sadistic personality traits, rather than obedience and conformity pressures or situational factors. This fits into a long-standing debate in psychology, referred to as the person-situation debate. Nowadays, however, psychologists generally agree that behavior is determined by an interrelationship between the person and the situation. One common illustration of the influence the situation has on behavior is the Stanford Prison Experiment, conducted by Phil Zimbardo (1972). In this study, college students were randomly assigned to the roles of either guards or prisoners. The guards wore uniforms and identified the prisoners by numbers, which helped to dehumanize them. Similar to Police Battalion 101, the guards were at first hesitant, but, eventually, many started to enjoy their new roles of authority and behaved sadistically towards the prisoners. Ultimately, according to Zimbardo's observations, the guards could be split into three types: lenient guards who never punished the prisoners, tough but fair guards who followed prison rules, and sadistic and dominant guards who invented creative ways of humiliating the prisoners and received pleasure from exercising power. Though planned to run two weeks, Zimbardo had to terminate the experiment after six days due to guards getting out of control. Interestingly, Browning (1992) found three similar groups in Reserve Police Battalion 101 as found by Zimbardo, including (1) a group of evaders, who assisted by taking prisoners to the trains, but never directly committed any killings; (2) a group of accommodators, who never refused an order when it came to mass killing, but never specifically volunteered for the task; and (3) a group of eager killers, who came to enjoy their role and their power over their victims.

The final point to make is regarding cognitive dissonance, when a person engages in an unpleasant activity, inconsistent with their beliefs and morals, so changes those views in order to be consistent with their behavior. The classic example is when a smoker convinces themself that there is nothing wrong with smoking so that their views and behavior are in harmony. The theory states that mental discomfort is caused when we behave in a way that is incongruent with our beliefs; therefore, either the behavior or the belief must change in order to lessen the discomfort. A well-known study by Festinger and Carlsmith (1959) showed that students would convince themselves they had enjoyed a tedious task if they had accepted a small sum of money for telling others it was enjoyable. In contrast, those who accepted a large sum of money for telling others the boring task was enjoyable felt no need to change their attitude. The implication is that those who accepted a small sum of money were unable to justify their lying behavior, therefore changed their beliefs unconsciously as they did not want to see themselves as liars. On the other hand, those who accepted a large sum of money were able to justify their lying behavior, so felt no discomfort.

Future studies demonstrated that induced compliance is especially likely to cause a person to change their attitude when their behavior had caused damaging consequences for another person (Cooper & Fazio, 1984). In some studies, when participants caused harm to another person (e.g., by administering electric shocks, such as in Milgram's experiments), their attitude towards the person changed (e.g., claiming the victim deserved their punishment; Brock & Buss, 1962). This is an example of the just world hypothesis (Lerner, 1980), when people convince themselves that victims deserve their suffering so that they can continue believing the world is a fair place in which to live. Herbert (1998, p. 112, as cited in Newman, 2002) applied this to the Holocaust, explaining that antisemitism during the war increased in Germany in part because people thought "there must be just cause behind the persecution of the Jews, since anyone getting this kind of punishment could certainly not be entirely innocent."

By using these findings to shed light on the psychology of the perpetrators of the Holocaust, it suggests that further acts of genocide would have led to increased dehumanization of the victims. Furthermore, given that members of Police Battalion 101 were explicitly given the option to step aside during the massacre of Jews, it means the perpetrators would have felt even greater need to justify their behavior and to commit to the belief that Jews were a threat to Germany. This would be the only way for them to live comfortably with what they had done. Like those who accepted the offer to lie in exchange for a small sum of money in Festinger and Carlsmith's study, members of Police Battalion 101 knew they could have resisted the offer to kill, so had to convince themselves that their actions were righteous to avoid a state of cognitive dissonance. The fact that officers consumed large amounts of alcohol before and after mass killings suggests further that they did not kill simply due to being rampant anti-semites, as claimed by Goldhagen (1996).[1] Major Trapp, commander of Police Battalion 101, was reported to have wept after the killing of 1500 Jews in Józefów on July 13, 1942, and to have said, "Man, ... such jobs don't suit me. But orders are orders ... If this Jewish business is ever avenged on earth, then have mercy on us Germans" (Browning, 1992, p. 83).

Arguably one of the most vivid and striking instances of cognitive dissonance can be found in Browning's *Nazi Policy, Jewish Workers, German Killers* (2000). The book contains extracts from a series of letters penned by a German soldier to his wife while stationed in Lithuania during 1941. Initially, upon commencing his service, he expressed disbelief in receiving orders to execute civilians and showed empathy towards terrorized Jewish civilians. He even shared accounts of his own benevolence, recounting how he offered bread to starving Jews whenever he could. Eight weeks into his deployment to Lithuania, he wrote to his wife again, confessing that he and his men had shot and killed 150 Jews, including women and children. In this letter, the soldier pleaded with his wife to never tell their daughter about his actions, clearly feeling a sense of shame for what he had participated in. However, only nine weeks after this, he wrote again to his wife, this time boasting proudly over executions and providing gruesome details in delight. He even claimed to have filmed one of the executions and said, "In the future my film will be a document and of great interest to our children" (Browning, 2000, p.154). By this point, there was no hint of shame remaining, and he had convinced himself that the people he was killing were the enemy. It is an astounding example of how quickly one's mind and views can shift in order to protect one from seeing themselves as monstrous. After all, no one is the villain in their

---

[1] Alcohol desensitizes, acting as a coping mechanism.

own story, even if it means reconstructing reality in a fictitious and self-serving manner.

The aim of this chapter was to provide some examples of how social processes contribute to human behavior, especially in cases of extreme political atrocities, and not just personality traits or moral foundations. There is a powerful tendency for people to conform to the behavior of their group and to justify their behavior. Importantly, personality appears to have less of a significant influence on behavior in extreme situations than it does in ordinary ones. In unordinary instances, people are typically more likely to follow the norms of the group. Mass killings of racial, ethnic, and religious groups have occurred throughout human history and are not confined to the horrors of World War Two. In the 1990s alone, there were acts of genocide committed in front of the world in Bosnia, Kosovo, and Rwanda. It is tempting to pin these atrocities on dispositional factors (e.g., sadism) related to the perpetrators and to leave it at that, but that will not help us identify the social processes that may contribute to future genocides.

Lastly, I want to point out that the arguments made in this chapter in no way exculpate the perpetrators of mass genocide. While it is important to understand the worst of human behavior to identify signs in future cases, we must remember that there is a difference between explaining and condoning behavior. Indeed, even in the studies presented, free-will and individual differences were still at play. There were some who refused to conform to the group in Asch's studies and individuals who did not comply with the orders given in Milgram's experiments, even if they were a minority. Therefore, even in extreme situations, with apparent peer pressure and orders from authority, individuals should still be held responsible for their actions. I would also like to point out that the contents of *Ordinary Men* focus on explaining the behavior of those who actually carried out the killings, not those who gave the orders. When it comes to explaining the behavior and motives of those at the top of the Nazi hierarchy, such as Himmler and Hitler, there is clear evidence of psychopathologies and extreme personality traits (e.g., narcissism, psychopathy, RWA, SDO) that rendered them devoid of feelings of empathy and focused them on mass destruction (Tudoroiu, 2017). Indeed, once Germany was losing the war, Hitler's response was to increase the mass killings and to leave nothing in Germany of value to the Allied powers, despite the damage it would do to the German people. Therefore, in spite of the claims he made that he would be Germany's savior, the choices he made ensured he would only ever cause devastation. After reading this text, individuals should not feel as though they are constrained by their temperamental proclivities or directed solely by situational variables. Instead, they should realize that there is always the opportunity to learn, to grow, and to do good in the world.

# Summary

Behavior results from an interaction between personality and situational variables, including peer pressure and obedience to authority. In some circumstances, individuals who would not otherwise behave violently may commit political atrocities. Christopher Browning's *Ordinary Men* (1992) provides an example of this, where war crimes were committed by individuals who believed they could behave violently without facing consequences.

# References

Brock, T. C., & Buss, A. H. (1962). Dissonance, aggression, and evaluation of pain. *The Journal of Abnormal and Social Psychology, 65*(3), 197–202. https://doi.org/10.1037/h0048948

Browning, C. R. (1992). *Ordinary men: Reserve police battalion 101 and the final solution in Poland*. Harper Perennial.

Browning, C. R. (2000). *Nazi Policy Jewish Workers German Killers*. Cambridge University Press. https://doi.org/10.1017/CBO9780511665301

Chamberlain, S. (2004). The nature and care of the future master race. *The Journal of Psychohistory, 31*, 367–394.

Cooper, J., & Fazio, R. H. (1984). A new look at dissonance theory. *Advances in Experimental Social Psychology, 17*, 229–266. https://doi.org/10.1016/S0065-2601(08)60121-5

DeMause, L. (2002). *The emotional life of nations*. Karnac.

Festinger, L., & Carlsmith, J. M. (1959). Cognitive consequences of forced compliance. *The Journal of Abnormal and Social Psychology, 58*(2), 203–210. https://doi.org/10.1037/h0041593

Goldhagen, D. J. (1996). *Hitler's willing executioners: Ordinary Germans and the holocaust*. Alfred A. Knopf.

Lerner, M. J. (1980). *The belief in a just world: A fundamental delusion*. Plenum.

Newman, L. S. (2002). What is a "social-psychological" account of perpetrator behavior? In L. S. Newman & R. Erber (Eds.), *Understanding genocide: The social psychology of the holocaust*. The Oxford University Press.

Rowold, K. (2013). Johanna Haarer and Frederic Truby king: When is a baby-care manual an instrument of National Socialism? *German History, 31*(2), 181–203.

Tudoroiu, T. (2017). *The revolutionary totalitarian personality: Hitler, Mao, Castro, and Chávez*. Springer.

Zimbardo, P. G. (1972). Pathology of imprisonment. *Society, 9*(6), 4–6.

# 15

# Final Thoughts: Explaining Ideological Possession

**Abstract** This final chapter attempts to bring together the previously discussed points to explain what factors might lead to ideological possession and offers some suggestions to counteract this phenomenon.

**Keywords** Personality • Political orientations • Ideological possession

Swiss psychiatrist, Carl Jung (1958), believed the human psyche has a natural tendency towards wholeness and balance, and that psychological problems arise when this balance is disrupted. One way in which this can occur is through the extreme identification with a particular ideology, or archetype embodying the principles of that ideology, leading to what Jung called "ideological possession." When this phenomenon occurs, it leads to a loss of objectivity, a sense of righteous conviction, and a tendency to demonize those with different beliefs. In some cases, the person or group becomes so deeply invested in their beliefs that it takes on a cult-like or fanatical quality. When individuals or groups become ideologically possessed, they may see opposing political viewpoints as not just different, but as fundamentally wrong or even evil.

In political contexts, ideological possession can be particularly concerning as it can lead to polarization and even violence. For example,
political divisions in the United States have intensified in recent years,
with both the left and the right demonizing those who hold opposing
viewpoints. Wang et al. (2020) argue that social media has accelerated
echo-chamber emergence and entrenchment in certain political views, as
well as further radicalized individuals with extreme ideologies since they
are not being exposed to contrary opinions. On the far-right, there has
been a rise in groups espousing anti-immigrant, white nationalist, and
antisemitic views in various parts of the world. Similarly, the far-left has
produced extremist groups, such as Antifa, believing in the absolute correctness of their ideology, to the point of refusing to engage in democratic
processes.

As outlined in Chap. 14, one historical example of political ideological
possession is the rise of the Nazi Party in Germany. Their nationalist, rac-
ist, and antisemitic beliefs were based on the notion of Aryan superiority.
Under Adolf Hitler's leadership, the party became convinced that their
ideology was the only legitimate one, and all other perspectives were
wrong or even dangerous. Consequently, this led to the persecution of
Jews, homosexuals, disabled people, and other marginalized groups, with
millions of people killed in the Holocaust. Chapter 14 discussed some of
the social factors, such as conformity and obedience to authority, that can
facilitate such atrocities. Furthermore, Chap. 12 explained the roots of
authoritarianism that may lead one to hold prejudicial views, and
Chap. 10 provided some examples of predispositions interlinked with
personality traits that may have one cling to order and policies that ostra-
cize out-groups. Even today, the tragedy of the Nazi regime should serve
as a stark warning over the dangers of ideological possession in politics.

As illustrated in this text, personality traits may be related to proneness
for ideological possession in political contexts. For instance, people who
score high on measures of dogmatism and need for closure may be more
susceptible to ideological possession because they are less likely to engage
in critical thinking and may be more likely to cling to absolute beliefs,
rather than acknowledging the complexity and nuance of political issues.
Both of these concepts have been linked to Openness in the Big Five
Model of personality, with those scoring low in Openness being less likely

to consider alternative viewpoints or challenge their own beliefs (Mondak & Halperin, 2008; Onraet et al., 2011). Furthermore, those who score high on measures of authoritarianism may be more prone to ideological possession because they are more likely to conform to the beliefs of their political leaders or party, rather than critically evaluating those beliefs. While these personality traits do not necessarily determine an individual's political beliefs, they may influence how individuals process and respond to political information and engage in political discourse.

Jung (1958) believed that combating ideological possession required one to become more self-aware and to engage in the process of individuation (the process of becoming more whole and balanced). This includes one becoming more conscious of their own biases, so that they might better understand their own vulnerabilities and limitations and have more control over them. To counteract ideological possession, several specific suggestions can be made. Firstly, practicing critical thinking by questioning one's own beliefs, carefully evaluating the source of political information, and striving to assess arguments and evidence more objectively. Secondly, seeking out diverse perspectives to broaden one's understanding of political issues and challenge assumptions. Thirdly, avoiding demonizing opposing views to enable constructive dialogue, empathy, and finding common ground. Ultimately, combatting ideological possession begins with understanding one's self, as well as their natural temptations, that may be a part of their personality, and then a willingness to challenge one's self and seek out engagement with different views. As said at the end of Chap. 14, though people's behavior may be interlinked with personality dispositions, early emerging characteristics or situational factors do not determine the entire course of their life, as individuals have the ability to evolve and take control of their own growth.

# References

Jung, C. G. (1958). *The undiscovered self*. Little, Brown, and Company.
Mondak, J. J., & Halperin, K. D. (2008). A framework for the study of personality and political behaviour. *British Journal of Political Science, 23*, 443–455. https://doi.org/10.1038/s41593-020-0600-3

Onraet, E., Van Hiel, A., Roets, A., & Cornelis, I. (2011). The closed mind: 'Experience' and 'cognition' aspects of openness to experience and need for closure as psychological bases for right-wing attitudes. *European Journal of Personality, 25*(3), 184–197. https://doi.org/10.1002/per.775

Wang, X., Sirianni, A. D., Tang, S., Zheng, Z., & Fu, F. (2020). Public discourse and social network echo chambers driven by socio-cognitive biases. *Physical Review X, 10*(4), 041042. https://doi.org/10.1103/PhysRevX.10.041042

# Index[1]

[1] Note: Page numbers followed by 'n' refer to notes.

The manufacturer's authorised representative in the EU is Springer
Nature Customer Service Centre GmbH, Europaplatz 3, 69115 Heidelberg,
Germany. If you have any concerns regarding our products, please
contact ProductSafety@springernature.com

Printed and bound by CPI Group (UK) Ltd, Croydon, CR0 4YY

24/04/2026

02096315-0012